INDIA THROUGH PEOPLE

25 GAME CHANGERS

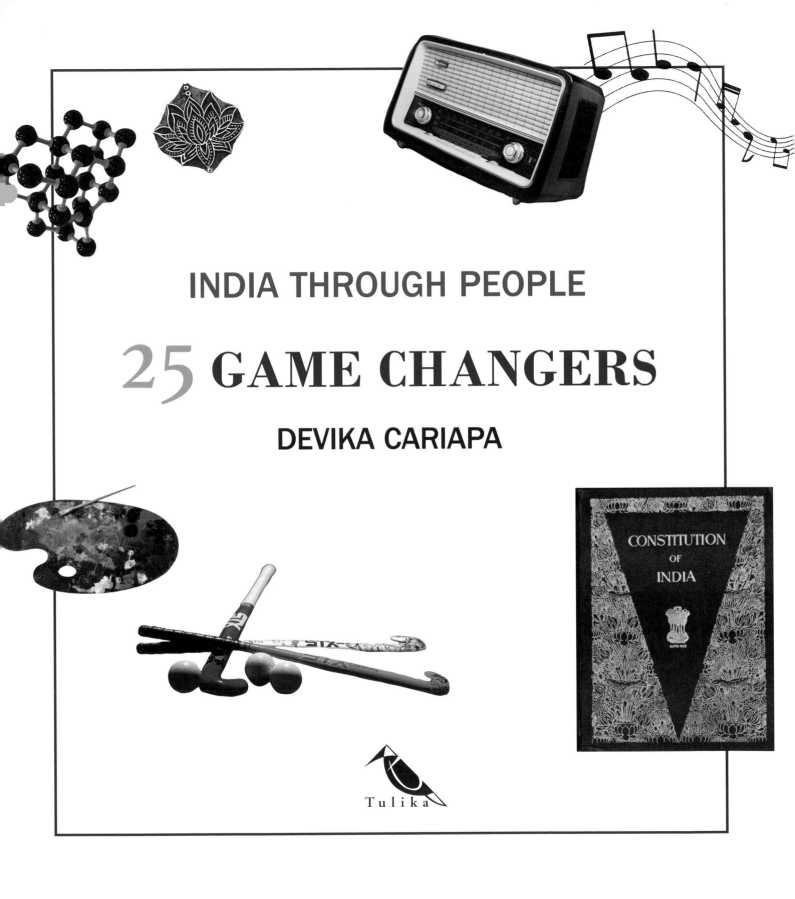

INDIA THROUGH PEOPLE

25 GAME CHANGERS

DEVIKA CARIAPA

CONSTITUTION
OF
INDIA

Tulika

CONTENTS

For Pa, greatest of adventurers
and Mama, most engaging of storytellers
With love and gratitude

India Through People: 25 Game Changers

ISBN 978-93-89203-17-2

First published in India, 2019

Published by
Tulika Publishers, 305 Manickam Avenue, TTK Road, Alwarpet, Chennai 600 018, India
email reachus@tulikabooks.com *website* www.tulikabooks.com

Printed by
Sudarsan Graphics, Chennai, India

Our thanks to A. R. Venkatachalapathy, Arna Seal, Arunava Sen, N. Sudarshan, Rubin D'Cruz, Sadanand Menon and Sudipto Mondal for their valuable feedback on some chapters, and to Aliya Aziz for help with Urdu.

EDITORS: Deeya Nayar, Radhika Menon

EDITORIAL TEAM: Kinnari Acharya, Priya Krishnan, Purnasneha S.

COVER DESIGN & COLLAGES: Aparna Chivukula

TIMELINE VISUALS: Roshini Pochont

DESIGN: Radhika Menon

DESIGN TEAM: Aparna Chivukula, Roshini Pochont, Siva Chidamabaram

JOURNEYS THAT SHAPED A NATION

INDIA AS A COUNTRY is something of a wonder. Think about it. So many ethnic groups, religions and cultures, and hundreds of languages. One-sixth of humanity squeezed into an area best described as a subcontinent! In recent history, this vast nation has been buffeted by revolutionary change – shaking off 200 years of colonial rule, examining and shedding age-old social customs, absorbing influences from a fast changing and more connected world, to emerge as an independent, modern nation. Shaping all of this have been some extraordinary people.

We call them the game changers. Men and women who, with their ideas and actions, left a radical imprint on the course of the country. They broke taboos, set trends and forged new paths, often at personal cost and against impossible odds. Any time of transformation typically brings to the fore outstanding achievers, and to pick some over others is naturally difficult. Twenty-five of them are in this book. They were all born after 1850, and represent diverse fields and parts of the country. You will recognise some of them at once, some may be unfamiliar. Names of other great contemporaries appear along the way, giving a wider picture of the age.

It is useful to remember that many of these people lived in very different times, with different kinds of issues to deal with. They should be seen through that viewpoint, and not from our present outlook. For their time, they were bold and visionary. They were iconic achievers, not perfect human beings as we often expect our idols to be. They made mistakes and changed their minds. Some are criticised today for things they said or did, their ideas challenged – but we can thank them for creating the space that makes it possible for us to do that!

Through their individual journeys, they tell the story of the world's largest and most diverse democracy.

রবীন্দ্রনাথ ঠাকুর

RABINDRANATH TAGORE

1861–1941

As his country awoke from the
oppression of colonial rule to call for political freedom,
Tagore cut a distinctive path. His appeal was for individual liberty,
for freedom from irrational traditions and divisions of religion and
society. At a time of nationalistic fervour, he asked for a 'world family'
to share the best of humanity's offerings. His life spanned the cusp
of two centuries, and his literary genius left its mark on both with
thousands of his poems, stories, songs and plays. His impact on
Bengali speakers, in particular, is matched by few in other
language groups in the world.

"SCHOOL DROPOUT WINS Nobel Prize!" screamed the headlines.

Or they should have on 10 December 1913, when Rabindranath Tagore was awarded the Nobel Prize — the first non-European to get the prize for literature and the first Asian to win any sort of Nobel.

Tagore was indeed a school dropout. How did he make such a mark in literature?

He belonged to an extremely wealthy and intellectual family that had led the progressive Brahmo Samaj movement. His father and grandfather were scholars of Persian and Arabic. There were mathematicians, musicians and artists. Sanskrit texts were read and discussed in the house quite casually. And at least one of his sisters was a famous author. By the age of eight, the young Rabi was already writing poetry. After the freewheeling, brilliant atmosphere of his home, the schoolrooms of the British education system stifled the boy.

Much to his family's dismay, he rebelled and refused to attend school. His father was appalled but eventually agreed to the whim of his youngest child. Then, in a strange twist, Tagore began to use his freedom from school to go back to studying! He read everything he could, gathering knowledge from every source, tuning his mind to be open, to use reason and to question even the most orthodox beliefs.

He poured out his radical social and political ideas in poetry, novels, music, essays and plays in both Bengali and English. He wrote in support of the peasants, against the caste system, against communalism and the oppression of women. He opposed violence no matter what the cause, as also superstitions and meaningless rituals.

By the early 20th century, he was not only one of the most learned men in India but also a world famous poet. He travelled round the globe, interacting with major intellectuals of the day, such as W. B. Yeats, Albert Einstein and Bertrand Russell. At his lectures, awestruck crowds hung on to every word of this striking prophet-like figure with the long robes, flowing beard and piercing eyes.

Back home, his ideas had a major influence on the leaders of India's freedom movement, including his close friends, Mahatma Gandhi, Jawaharlal Nehru and Subhas Chandra Bose. Sometimes, though, his ideas clashed with popular opinion. For instance, he thought Gandhiji's idea of spinning on the charkha every day was

"Patriotism cannot be our final spiritual shelter; my refuge is humanity. I will not buy glass for the price of diamonds, and I will never allow patriotism to triumph over humanity as long as I live."
Rabindranath Tagore

"He [Tagore] has been India's internationalist par excellence, believing and working for international cooperation, taking India's message to other countries and bringing their message to his own people."
Jawaharlal Nehru

rather old fashioned — he wanted India to take up more modern ways to deal with poverty. And during the Non-cooperation movement, he was upset that students left schools and colleges with no thought about their future education.

While Gandhiji himself never let their differences of opinion interfere with their friendship, Tagore gained some critics.

He believed that borders between countries should never stop anyone from appreciating the best of what other cultures had to offer. This meant that while he criticised the British Raj, he was not afraid of appreciating the finer points of Western culture. Of course, this did not go down too well in the country. It was the height of the freedom struggle and many felt he was not being patriotic enough. Tagore, although greatly respected, began to feel a bit isolated. But he was unafraid to go it alone with his convictions. As he wrote in one of the most powerful songs of the freedom movement, and one of Gandhiji's personal favourites, 'Ekla cholo re' — "If no one heeds your call, then walk alone..."

Tagore was convinced that the key to India's progress was a completely new pattern of education. He wanted children to gain knowledge through observation and experiment, and to be able to examine ideas through reasoning. So he founded a very unique school, Shantiniketan, where boys and girls sat together under trees and learnt from nature. No classrooms or textbooks or exams. They celebrated the seasons and worked with their hands like peasants and craftsmen. They read and discussed world affairs, mingled with visiting foreign artists and writers, and gave opinions freely. There was art, music, dance, theatre, and physical activity — girls even learnt judo, almost a century ago!

But it was a struggle to sustain. The story goes that when he heard of the Nobel Prize, he was in a meeting on funding for the school plumbing — and Tagore announced to the committee, "Money for the drains has probably been found!"

His dream for India can be best summed up in one of his most famous poems:

> Where the mind is without fear and the head is held high
> Where knowledge is free
> Where the world has not been broken up into fragments by narrow domestic walls
> Into that heaven of freedom ... let my country awake.

"For the Bengali public, Tagore has been, and remains, an altogether exceptional literary figure, towering over all others. His poems, songs, novels, short stories, critical essays, and other writings have vastly enriched the cultural environment in which hundreds of millions of people live in the Bengali-speaking world, whether in Bangladesh or in India."

Amartya Sen, Nobel Laureate economist and philosopher, 2011

"In a country, where hatred of neighbours is taught by religion, where a man invites hell's wrath by drinking water from the glass of another, when one race is redeemed by humiliating another, then degradations and insults await the people of that country ... We have divided ourselves, and, since we understand difference more than unity, we will never rid ourselves of slavery and piteous humiliation."

Rabindranath Tagore

"I am proud of my humanity when I can acknowledge the poets and artists of other countries as my own. Let me feel with unalloyed gladness that all the great glories of man are mine."

obel prize
n literature

1913

1861

Born in Jorashanko, Kolkata, on 7 May. Growing up in the huge mansion of the Tagore (Thakur, in Bengali) family, he is left to himself for long hours of fantasy and imaginative play.

1873

His father takes him on a trip to the Himalayas for several months. Conversations with his philosopher father, being with nature, and reading books on great lives, history, astronomy and science leave a lasting impression.

1877

Writes his first set of poems under the pseudonym 'Bhanushingho' in the Brajabuli dialect — these are taken to be long-lost literary finds by critics! After this, begins to publish poems, stories and plays in his own name.

1878

After home-schooling for some years, goes to Brighton, England, for formal education. Does a brief stint later at University College, London, to study law.

1881

Writes *Balmiki Protibha*, his first play. It is enacted in the Jorashanko house by the family, with Tagore as Balmiki. Bengali women so far confined at home act on stage for the first time. The play impresses eminent writer Bankim Chandra Chattopadhyay who is in the audience.

1890s

Sent to manage the family estates in Shelaidaho (now in Bangladesh). Sees first-hand the feudalism of landlords as well as the poverty and backwardness of peasants, with Muslims the worst off. Also becomes acquainted with the songs of bauls, the wandering minstrels. All this deeply influences him and shows up in his political and creative writings.

Begins his most productive literary phase with major works *Visarjan, Chitrangada, Manasi, Shonar Tori...*

1900s

Founds Vishwa Bharati at Shantiniketan, which would even now be considered a very inclusive, multicultural educational institution — path-breaking at the time for being coeducational.

In 1911, his 'Jana Gana Mana' in Sanskritised Bengali, set to music also by him, is sung at the Kolkata session of the Indian National Congress. This first stanza of his longer Brahmo song 'Bharata Bhagya Bidhata' is adopted as India's national anthem in 1950.

The West is impressed by the English translations of his poetry in *Gitanjali*. Tagore starts lecturing and reading from his works in Europe, the Americas, and East Asia. Becomes an eloquent spokesperson for Indian independence.

Awarded the Nobel Prize in Literature for *Gitanjali* in 1913.

In 1915, he is awarded British knighthood. Returns it in 1919 as a protest against the Jallianwalla Bagh massacre.

Meets Gandhi for the first time also in 1915. From now till Tagore's death in 1941, the two are in regular touch through meetings, letters and telegrams. They discuss subjects like truth, freedom, democracy, courage, education, and the future of humanity.

1920s

By now he is a pioneering literary figure, renowned for his ceaseless innovations in poetry, prose, drama and music. In his 60s, he takes up painting and produces works that place him among India's foremost contemporary artists — debuts with an exhibition in Paris.

1930

Has a historic meeting with Albert Einstein at his home near Berlin, where they talk about science and religion.

1941

After his numerous poems, stories and plays, and almost 2000 songs, in the last poem just before his death he writes, "Today my sack is empty. I have given completely what I had to give..."

रखमाबाई

RAKHMABAI

1864–1955

Sati, child marriage, killing of newborn girls,
cruelty to widows… These were only some of the horrors society
had imposed on women. Apart from demanding complete obedience
and denying them an education that might encourage them to think.
Reform movements had started in the 19th century, but they were
mostly helmed by upper class men. In this milieu arrived young
Rakhmabai – questioning, insisting on rights, determined to study and
to get justice. The furore she created brought about the Age
of Consent Act – a first step which showed women that the
fight for equality was theirs to take forward.

ON 26 JUNE 1885, readers of *The Times of India*, Mumbai, were in for a shock. There were knocked over teacups and probably a few cases of choking on the hot liquid, as they read a letter to the editor entitled 'Infant Marriage and Enforced Widowhood' by someone who signed herself as 'A Hindu Lady'.

It was a long letter. And the contents of it were so bold and outspoken for their time that it set off a chain of events — clashes in the British and Indian press, arguments among social reformers and nationalists, and a confused judiciary. Many twists and turns later, the chain finally ended with the highest authority in the British Empire, Queen Victoria herself!

A moving paragraph sat at the heart of the letter: "Sir, I am one of those unfortunate Hindu women, whose hard lot it is to suffer the unnameable miseries entailed by the custom of early marriage. This wicked practice has destroyed the happiness of my life. It comes between me and that thing which I prize above all others — study and mental cultivation…"

But who was this 'Hindu Lady'? And why did she talk with such passion on the subject? It all goes back to March 1884 and the case of 'Bhikaji vs Rakhmabai'.

Rakhmabai was born in 1864. Her mother, Jayantibai Save, was a child widow who remarried Dr Sakharam Arjun, a well known doctor and social reformer of Mumbai. At age 11, Rakhmabai was married to 19-year-old Dadaji Bhikaji, but continued to live with her parents, as was the custom, till older.

Bhikaji turned out to be totally disinterested in education or a responsible job. Living recklessly and in bad company, he ruined his health and got into debt. In the meanwhile, Rakhmabai was encouraged by her parents to educate herself, although it was unusual for women those days. She read books from the Free Church Mission Library, taught herself English and interacted with the Europeans and social reformers who called on her father. Her mother took her to Arya Samaj and Prarthana Samaj meetings. There grew in her a strong desire to do something for women in society by improving on her own education.

When she turned 19, Dadaji demanded that she move into his home and start being a wife. Rakhmabai refused! She had no intention of giving up her precious education for a marriage forced on her as a child to a thoroughly unreliable man.

"You, gentlemen, anxiously long for the regeneration of India. If arts and sciences flourish, if trade and industry progress among our people, you think everything will come right. India will prosper. But do you seriously believe … that such a happy state of things is possible when you allow boys and girls to be fathers and mothers before they are hardly out of their teens? … Do you think that the sons and daughters of such parents, who want strength of body and mind themselves, will be capable of achieving the bright future which … you fondly anticipate for them?"
Rakhmabai's letter in *The Times of India*

"The government advocated education and emancipation but when a woman refused to 'be a slave' the government comes to break her spirit, allowing its law to become [the] instrument of riveting her chains."
Pandita Ramabai, social reformer

Imagine the scandal this created in the conservative 19th century, when girls were not expected to question the rules set for them by society!

A miffed Dadaji went to court, and the judges ordered Rakhmabai to join her husband or spend six months in jail. She declared that she would rather go to jail than live with her wastrel of a husband.

As the case dragged on, the letters from 'A Hindu Lady' began to appear in *The Times of India*. They grabbed public attention. People began to discuss the evil of child marriage and the right of women to decide their own affairs. Social reformers like the journalist Behramji Malabari wrote to bring attention to the case, even forming a Rakhmabai Defence Committee. But conservative Hindus and some nationalists were angry, declaring that the colonial state had no right to interfere with their customs. There were heated debates in the British and Indian press.

When one of the mystery letters appeared in *The Times*, London, it was finally revealed that the eloquent author, the 'Hindu Lady', was none other than Rakhmabai! She then sent a final heartfelt appeal to Queen Victoria on behalf of all the suffering child brides of India. The queen responded by dissolving the marriage. Dadaji sulked but was happy with a payout of a substantial 2000 rupees. And Rakhmabai was finally free.

With the support of well-wishers, she left for England to study medicine. She returned to India as one of the very first Indian women medical doctors, taking up the post as the Chief Medical Officer of the Women's Hospital in Surat. Her wish to serve her less fortunate sisters had finally come true.

There was more. With the huge publicity around her case, the government was forced to enact the Age of Consent Bill, which changed the age at which a girl could 'consent' to cohabit with her husband from 10 to 12 years.

A very small concession. But Rakhmabai had opened up the possibility that women could question and change age-old customs — that they had choices.

"The extremists are afraid of books and pens. The power of education frightens them ... This is why they killed 14 innocent students in the recent attack in Quetta. And that is why they kill female teachers ... Today I am focusing on women's rights and girls' education because they are suffering the most."
Malala Yousafzai, Nobel Peace Prize winner and human rights activist, 2013

"The report revealed that worldwide, an estimated 650 million girls and women alive were married before their 18th birthday and, globally, the total number of girls married in childhood is estimated at 12 million per year."
Unicef, 2019

NOT WITHOUT CONSENT

1864

Born to a Marathi family on 22 November in Mumbai. Loses her father two years later.

1872

Her mother, married at 14 herself and widowed at 17, remarries Sakharam Arjun, physician and social activist — widow remarriage is allowed in their Suthar community.

1875

Eleven-year-old Rakhmabai is married to Dadaji Bhikaji but is to stay with her parents until she comes of age.

1876

Refuses to move to her husband's house because she disapproves of his wayward ways. Continues to educate herself. Sakharam supports her decision.

1884

Dadaji finally sends a legal notice and petitions the Bombay High Court to direct his wife to start living with him.

1885

The first letter by 'A Hindu Lady' appears in *The Times of India* — a plea against child marriage and to pay heed to the problems of Hindu women.

Despite criticism from traditionalists, the 'Bhikaji vs Rakhmabai' case is ruled in Rakhmabai's favour, saying she had been married in "helpless infancy" and so should not be forced to honour it.

1886

Public excitement around the case. Appeal and retrial.

1887

Judgement orders Rakhmabai "to go live with her husband or face six months of imprisonment".

Social reformers like Behramji Malabari and Pandita Ramabai form the Rakhmabai Defence Committee.

Rakhmabai's letter to the editor appears in *The Times*, London.

As a final resort, she writes to Queen Victoria, who signs a special order and overrules the court order.

END CHILD MARRIAGE NOW

ROYAL MARATHA ENTERTAINMENT PRESENTS

TANNISHTHA CHATTERJEE

DOCTOR RAKHMABAI

A FILM BY ANANTH NARAYAN MAHADEVAN

A DR. SWAPNA PATKER PRODUCTION

SHE WAS THE FIRST...

> "In the prevailing customs ...a woman [cannot] deny to live with [her husband] even on reasonable grounds.
>
> He may ill-treat her, beat her, drive her away a thousand times, keep her without food, but she must submit to her lot and stay with him (if he keeps her) till she dies a natural death or is killed by him, her sole lord and master...
>
> (We women have become) timid, languid, melancholy, sickly, devoid of cheerfulness, and therefore incapable of communicating to others ...we have naturally come to look down upon ourselves...[but] I... wished to do something, if in my power, to ameliorate our present suffering."
>
> *- From Rakhmabai's Letters in the Times of India, 1887. Rakhmabai was married as a child and refused to live with her husband or consummate her marriage, even though a court ordered her to.* #The 'Age' of Agency

1888

The marriage is dissolved with Rs 2000 as compensation for Dadaji.

1889

With support from Edith Pechey Phipson and other activists, she goes to study medicine in London, as well as in Edinburgh, Glasgow and Brussels.

1891

The British-Indian government passes the Age of Consent Act, influenced by Rakhmabai's case.

1894

Rakhmabai graduates as Doctor of Medicine from the London School of Medicine for Women.

Becomes the third Indian woman to get a medical degree in Western medicine, after Anandi Gopal Joshi and Kadambini Ganguly.

1895

Returns to India and wants to help women. Becomes Chief Medical Doctor at the Women's Hospital, Surat. Starts her career in medicine, though she still faces hostility from parts of society.

1918

Joins the Zenana (Women's) State Hospital in Rajkot.

1929

Retires after a career of 35 years. Moves back to Mumbai. Publishes a pamphlet on 'Purdah — the need for its abolishment' about the plight of young widows in India.

મહાત્મા ગાંધી

MAHATMA GANDHI

1869–1948

Dimmed by the overpowering aura that surrounds
Mahatma Gandhi today, and almost forgotten, is the brilliance
of this political strategist who led India to freedom. Living through
some of the most violent times in history and having seen British
imperialism for himself on two continents, he realised that the nature
of the fight would have to change. So, he turned to the concept of
ahimsa or non-violence and renewed it as a potent, ethical
political tool. With this, he empowered millions of ordinary
people to join the struggle – and showed the world the
power of mind over physical force.

THERE WAS ONCE A MAN who decided to take on the might of an empire.

The empire in question was huge. It covered almost a quarter of the earth, and it was said that the sun never set on it. You would assume that to challenge such an empire would take at least one commanding figure in sharp clothes, some shiny medals, and the backing of a strong, well equipped army.

Instead, as unlikely as it seems, the challenger was a small-made, somewhat shy person, who wore a simple dhoti and shawl and was armed with nothing more than the moral force he called 'satyagraha' — literally, truth (satya) force (agraha).

Growing up in Porbandar and Rajkot in Gujarat, Mohandas Karamchand Gandhi was, as he described himself, an average student with bad handwriting, who shirked physical activity and had a real fear of bullies, ghosts and demons! But from his earliest days, he had a very strong sense of right and wrong.

After studying law in England, Gandhi moved to work in South Africa. There, he gained first-hand experience of racial and colonial discrimination. In one — now famous — incident, he was thrown out of the first class compartment of a train despite having a ticket simply because a white person objected to sitting with him, a 'coloured' man. On that freezing night, spent shivering in the waiting room at Pietermaritzburg railway station, Gandhi decided to begin his fight against injustice and prejudice.

Two decades in South Africa shaped the person he was to become. It was here, working for the rights of the Indian community, that he finally overcame his fear of public speaking. He worked as lawyer, activist, newspaper editor and teacher, and even experimented with being a barber and washerman! He read widely and was influenced by the writings of John Ruskin to start the Phoenix settlement, a unique experiment in communal living where people of every faith and background lived and worked together, receiving equal wages for what they did.

When Gandhi came back to India in 1915, he jumped into the forefront of the freedom struggle with two very important ideas.

Travelling across India, he saw terrible poverty and people divided by caste and religion. He decided that there had to be a bridge between the elite who were

"The greatest omission in our 106-year history is undoubtedly that Mahatma Gandhi never received the Nobel Peace Prize."
Geir Lundestad, Secretary, Norwegian Nobel Committee, 2006

"Although Mahatma Gandhi was not awarded the Nobel Peace Prize ... the coveted honour has gone to several individuals who believed in and propagated the Gandhian philosophy of peace and non-violence globally. Barack Hussein Obama ... is the latest in this club of Gandhian followers to have been awarded the Nobel Peace Prize. Prominent followers in the recent past have been Nelson Mandela, Aung San Suu Kyi and the Dalai Lama."
Lalit K. Jha, journalist, 2009

fighting for freedom, and the downtrodden who believed they had no power to influence the way things were run.

He started by switching his Western clothes to the simple homespun dhoti and shawl of the Indian peasant. He began to eat frugally, mostly fruits and nuts. And he took up causes that had a direct impact on poor farmers, factory workers, and the so-called untouchables. More people began to identify with him, realising that they too could make a difference to the struggle for freedom. He quickly became an immensely popular leader. Many even regarded him a saint!

Then there was his radical idea of satyagraha. Gandhi realised that violence was a weapon easily defeated with yet more violence — a battle the British could easily win. A satyagrahi does not hit back but refuses to submit to injustice, waiting till the conscience of the oppressor is aroused to do the right thing. Based on the ancient Indian concept of ahimsa or non-violence, satyagraha believes that even the strongest physical force will eventually bend before the moral force of truth. Gandhi directed Indians to take on the powerful British Empire with resistance tactics such as strikes, refusal to pay taxes, not attending British-run schools and colleges, not using British manufactured goods, and not respecting their discriminatory laws. In other words, defy them by not cooperating with them!

How did that work against a high-handed rule?

During the famous Salt Satyagraha, an American journalist reported how police officials dealt with unarmed marchers trying to protest an unjust law that taxed a basic commodity like salt: "Scores of police rushed on the advancing marchers and rained blows on their heads with their lathis. Not one of the marchers raised an arm to fend off the blows ... I heard the sickening whacks of the clubs on unprotected skulls ... At times the spectacle of unresisting men being methodically bashed into bloody pulp sickened me so much that I had to turn away..."

In other words, satyagraha required courage and self-control. It was certainly not for the faint-hearted! Yet, millions of men and women came out to fight this non-violent battle.

In the end, the mighty British Empire had no choice but to do the right thing and grant India its freedom.

"Far from being a paragon of virtue, the Mahatma remained until his death a restless work in progress. Prone to committing what he called 'Himalayan blunders', he did not lose his capacity to learn from them, and to enlist his opponents in his search for a mutually satisfactory truth."
Pankaj Mishra, writer, 2018

"In my view, four aspects of Gandhi's legacy remain relevant, not just to India, but to the world.

First, non-violent resistance to unjust laws and/or authoritarian governments.

Second, the promotion of inter-faith understanding and religious tolerance.

Third, an economic model that does not ... pillage nature.

Fourth, courtesy in public debate and transparency in one's public dealings."
Ramachandra Guha, historian and biographer, 2013

God is Truth
The way to Truth
lies through Ahimsa
(non-violence,
Sabarmati
13 3/127   M.K.Gandhi

salt satyagraha

non-cooperation

"With this I'm
shaking the
foundations of the
British Empire."

M.K.Gandhi

BAPU OF THE NATION

1869

Born in Porbandar, Gujarat, on 2 October, which is now International Day of Non-Violence. The family moves to Rajkot when he is 5 years old. As a child he is "restless as mercury, either playing or roaming about".

1888–1894

Leaves for England to study at the University of London, and then law at the Inner Temple. Tries to be an English 'gentleman', and learns public speaking to overcome his shyness as a lawyer.

Goes to work in South Africa in 1893. Faces discrimination — has to sit on the floor in the bus, is thrown off a train in Pietermaritzburg, kicked off the footpath by a policeman...

In 1894, founds the Natal Indian Congress, a voice for Indians in South Africa.

1900s

Starts Phoenix Farm, Natal, in 1904, and *Indian Opinion*, a multilingual journal about injustice against Indians.

Leads the first satyagraha campaign in 1906, to protest the Black Act, in Transvaal. The idea of satyagraha and non-violence take shape.

1910s

With Herman Kallenbach, in 1910 sets up Tolstoy Farm, named after the Russian writer, with whom he corresponds about non-violent freedom from colonial rule. His ideas about Nai Talim, his 'new education' system, germinate.

In 1915, suspends his struggle in South Africa, returns to India. Rabindranath Tagore refers to Gandhi as Mahatma, 'Great Soul'.

Launches the Champaran Satyagraha in 1917, to protest injustice to farmers — rents are reduced, and compulsion to grow indigo is removed.

Helped by Vallabhbhai Patel, leads a signature campaign by peasants in Kheda, Gujarat, in 1918 for tax relief after floods and famine.

In 1919, organises a nationwide crusade against the repressive Rowlatt Act. Supports the Khilafat movement to create Hindu-Muslim unity in fighting the British. This is initially successful, but antagonises M. A. Jinnah who later insists on a separate country for Muslims.

1920s

Now a prominent leader of the Indian National Congress (INC), his Non-cooperation movement has a nationwide impact. People from all walks of life begin to join the freedom struggle. Shakes up the British rulers.

Sets up branches of INC all over India to spread the message of nationalism. Takes up social reform at the same time.

His Swadeshi movement — boycott of foreign goods and institutions, wearing khadi — hurts the British politically and economically.

Goes to jail in 1922, during which INC splits into two factions and Muslim leaders form their own groups.

Pushes for Purna Swaraj at the 1929 Lahore session of the INC. The Indian flag is unfurled.

1930s

INC declares 'Indian independence' on 26 January 1930.

On 12 March, leads a 388-km march from Sabarmati Ashram to Dandi to make salt — a symbolic act of defiance against state monopoly and taxing of a basic commodity. There are parallel marches all over India. About 300 die or are injured. The British government panics, imprisons around 60,000 people.

In 1931, Gandhi-Irwin Pact is signed, ending Civil Disobedience. Gandhi is invited to the Round Table Conference in London to discuss self-rule. At the second Round Table Conference, Muslims, the princes and the lowered castes ask for separate representation.

In 1932, goes on a fast-unto-death in Yerwada Jail, Pune, to protest creation of a separate electorate for the so-called untouchable caste. Leads to a compromise, the Poona Pact.

In 1938, opposes Subhas Chandra Bose as Congress president because he does not believe in non-violence. Bose resigns.

1940s

Launches the Quit India movement in August 1942 in Mumbai, with the call to "Do or Die" for freedom. Arrested again.

Despite their differences, Subhas Chandra Bose calls him "Father of the Nation" in a radio address from Singapore in 1944.

Travels to Noakhali in East Bengal in 1946, to quell Hindu-Muslim violence.

On 15 August 1947, the first day of Independence, Gandhi is on a 24-hour fast in Kolkata for Hindu-Muslim unity.

Assassinated on 30 January 1948 by Nathuram Godse, a Hindu radical who thinks Gandhi has given in to the Muslims. One million people line the route of his funeral cortege.

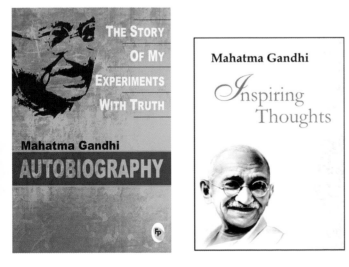

பெரியார் ஈ. வெ. ராமசாமி

PERIYAR E. V. RAMASAMY

1879–1973

To talk atheism in India was to wave
a red flag – and that was precisely Periyar's intention.
His radical voice jolted people out of unthinking prejudices and cruel
practices in the name of religion. He lashed out at every form of social
inequality, from strictures on women to the inhuman treatment of those
seen as untouchable. His Self-Respect movement resonated strongly
with the oppressed. He knew his hard-hitting views would never win
votes, so he opted out of political power. But he left a stamp
on Tamil Nadu politics that no politician
can ignore even today.

"HAVE CATS EVER FREED RATS? Have foxes ever liberated goats or chickens? Have Whites ever enriched Indians? ... We can be confident that women will never be emancipated by men."

In the 1920s, someone wrote this urgent message to women — an appeal to learn to fight for their own freedom, not depend on men to do the fighting for them.

Who was this radical feminist? It was, in fact, a man. His name was Erode Venkatappa Ramasamy Naicker.

Born in Erode, Tamil Nadu, the son of a prosperous businessman, Ramasamy dropped out of school in just the fourth grade to assist his father. But he had a keen mind. He learnt to observe, think independently, and to never accept an idea without questioning it first. He soon sent his Brahmin home tutors packing with his endless stream of logical arguments and criticisms of the scriptures!

The sharp-witted and rebellious boy decided to travel and discover things for himself. In Varanasi, while most saw a holy city, he saw destitute young widows begging in the streets, and half-burnt bodies being thrown into the Ganga.
He saw people steeped in poverty, ignorance and blind superstition, and how easily they were exploited in the name of religion by grasping priests. He himself was thrown out of the dining hall of a charitable home for not being of the right caste — meaning, Brahmin! Hungry, he was forced to eat scraps of food from the streets, once even from a funeral ritual.

These experiences had a great impact on him. Determined to change things, he returned home to a period of deep self-education, reading widely on modern, scientific thinking. Fired by the freedom struggle, he joined politics. In a short while, he was hailed as the hero of the Vaikom Satyagraha in which, after centuries of appalling discrimination, lowered castes were finally allowed to at least walk on the roads around the Mahadeva Temple at Vaikom, Kerala, if not enter inside it.

But it quickly became clear to Ramasamy that the Congress, even Gandhi, was not willing to go far enough in removing caste prejudice. He resigned from the Congress and distanced himself from Gandhi politically.

"If someone like me develops the desire for office, can I articulate the kind of issues and words that I now speak? Can anyone who seeks to capture political power speak in this manner? For example, I ask: 'Can a stone be god? Can god eat food? Does god need a wife? Why conduct the annual ritual of marriage for gods? Who benefits from all these?' Will the one who asks such questions get any votes? But if one does not ask questions in this manner will our foolish people understand a thing?"
Periyar

"Periyar was a democrat in a fundamental intellectual sense — he was open to differences, to worldviews different from his own, and believed in unfettered expression of ideas..."
Forward Press, 2017

From then on, Periyar, the 'Great Man', as he has come to be known, went down a far more radical path, parallel to the Independence movement.

To him, all social evils — the caste system, untouchability, child marriage and the low status of women — were due to blind faith in a man-made system called religion. He saw Brahmin priests as having enslaved society and monopolised learning, to leave the common people unable to think for themselves and open to exploitation. He was now a firm atheist. His only religion was humanism.

Aiming for a complete break with the past, Periyar launched the Self-Respect movement. Through dramatic rallies and hard-hitting, sometimes shocking, articles in his weekly publication *Kudi Arasu*, he urged people to fight the irrational, and to remember that their degradation was not due to karma or god but fellow human beings.

The movement conducted marriage ceremonies with no priests or religious rituals — men and women entered into an equal partnership of choice. Parents were told to bring up boys and girls as equals, with unisex names and clothes, and to encourage girls to learn boxing and martial arts. He wanted women empowered, to have the right to choose their partners, divorce, remarry, inherit property, use birth control. He even said that children should be brought up by the state, to leave women free to fulfil their potential.

You can imagine how shocking these views were at the time! Yet so popular, that the movement had over 117 branches across South India.

Periyar created a strong Tamil political identity. According to him, the concept of caste was imposed on the Dravida lands by the Sanskrit-speaking Aryan Brahmins of North India. He launched the Dravidar Kazahgam (DK) party demanding a separate state of Dravida Nadu. That was never to be. But from 1967 onwards, no party has ruled in Tamil Nadu that has not risen from the DK, no leader that does not claim Periyar as political mentor. Many of his ideas, particularly on caste based reservations, are now state government policy. To him, the uplift of a fellow human being and self-respect came first and foremost, before any religious or political affiliation.

"Forget god," he said, "think of man."

"Like all other anti-caste leaders in India, he believed in non-violence, and in this he was arguably more Gandhian than Gandhi himself. Periyar condemned violence during the 'Quit India' movement in 1942 as well as during the anti-Hindi agitations in Tamil Nadu in 1965...

...Periyar accepted the invitation of All India Radio to appeal to the people to remain calm in order to prevent any violence against Brahmins that might have broken out in Tamil Nadu following Gandhi's assassination (as it did in certain regions of Maharashtra)."
Punitha Pandiyan, editor of *Dalit Murasu*, 2017

"My ideology has been preached by Periyar too. There is no difference."
B. R. Ambedkar

There is no god.
There is no god.
There is no god at all.
He who invented god is a fool.
He who propagates god is a scoundrel.
He who worships god is a barbarian.

FORGET GOD;
THINK OF
MAN

Kudi Arasu

1879

Born on 17 September in Erode, Tamil Nadu, to a wealthy, upper class family.

1904

Visits Varanasi, and is shocked by the caste discrimination he sees and faces himself.

Comes back to settle into family life and work. Well known for managerial skills, expands family business.

1917

Becomes Chairman, Erode Municipality. Implements many welfare schemes such as better drainage and drinking water.

1919

Joins the Indian National Congress. He and his wife picket toddy shops, boycott shops selling foreign cloth, and promote the use of khadi.

1920s

Elected President of the Madras Presidency Congress Committee in 1922. Advocates reservation for lowered castes, and for so-called untouchables to enter temples.

In 1924, leads the Vaikom Satyagraha in Kerala and is imprisoned. Gandhi negotiates to allow lowered castes and so-called untouchables on the streets around the Mahadeva Temple for the first time. Periyar is upset with Gandhi for not insisting that they be allowed inside the temple too.

A Congress-funded school in Cheranmahadevi, Tirunelveli, insists on separate dining halls for non-Brahmin boys. To Periyar, this feels like a repeat of his Varanasi experience and he leaves the Congress.

Associates himself with the non-Brahmin Justice Party started by P. Theagaraya Chetty and T. M. Nair.

In 1925, starts publishing the Tamil weekly, *Kudi Arasu* ('Democracy').

In 1926, launches the Self-Respect movement to spread awareness among the oppressed classes to demand rights and fight religious exploitation.

At the First Provincial Self-Respect Conference in 1929 at Chengalpattu, he drops his caste name 'Naicker'.

1930s

Spends time travelling abroad during 1929–32. In his 3 months in Russia, is impressed by communism and believes it will sort out India's social ills. Becomes socialistic for a while.

In 1938, organises protests through the Justice Party against Hindi being made compulsory in Madras Presidency schools. Says it is a threat from North Indian Aryans to a progressive Dravidian culture. Raises slogan 'Tamil Nadu for Tamilians'.

Is given the title 'Periyar' at the Tamil Nadu Women's Conference in Chennai.

Elected President of the Justice Party in 1939.

PERIYAR
A POLITICAL BIOGRAPHY OF E.V. RAMASAMY
BALA JEYARAMAN

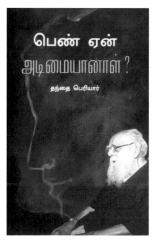

பெண் ஏன் அடிமையானாள்?
தந்தை பெரியார்

1940s

In 1944, renames the Justice Party as Dravidar Kazhagam (DK). Intensifies social reform work for the abolition of untouchability. Says, "What we need is a propagandist movement. Propagate, propagate, propagate, so that people change."

Holds the Blackshirts Conference in Madurai in 1946, as a sign of the darkness in the state.

On 15 August 1947, is not happy about Independence. Feels it will be an opportunity for the North to dominate the South. Is clear that the DK "does not enter legislatures. It does not try to form ministries. It does not contest elections."

His right-hand man, C. N. Annadurai leaves him in 1949 to form the Dravida Munnetra Kazhagam (DMK), wanting to take the movement into electoral politics.

1950s–1960s

Launches major anti-religion agitations in the mid-1950s, breaking idols of gods and burning images of Rama. Tours North India to encourage the backward castes there.

His movement results in de-Brahminising the Congress, and a non-Brahmin, K. Kamaraj, becomes the chief minister of Tamil Nadu. Periyar supports him and looks to him to fulfil his dreams of social justice — reservation, presence of non-Brahmins in political office, and modern institutional and industrial growth.

1973

At his last public meeting, calls for social equality as the only way to a dignified life. Dies soon after, aged 94.

বেগম রোকেয়া

BEGUM ROKEYA

1880–1932

Cornelia Sorabji of Pune was on her way
to becoming the first woman lawyer and, closer
home in Bengal, Sarala Devi Chaudhurani, one of
the first women graduates. But none of this filtered into the
confined zenana of Begum Rokeya's early life. She was simply
forbidden to study. And yet, snatching the makings of her own
education, she was a standout. Living her dream to write,
she authored some of the earliest feminist literature, while urging
Muslim women not to give in to the inequality forced on them.
She continues to be a feminist inspiration even now.

THERE IS A STORY CALLED *SULTANA'S DREAM,* set in a beautiful place called Ladyland. Here women run everything while men cook, clean, look after children, never come out in public. That's not all. The place has hydrogen powered flying cars, solar powered weaponry and cooking devices, and a water harvesting system that taps the clouds.

What is special about that, you may wonder. This science fiction with a feminist twist was written over a century ago! At that time, electricity was a novelty and people still went around in horse-drawn carriages. What's more, the author of this, one of the earliest pieces of science fiction writing in India, was a woman who had never been to school — Begum Rokeya Sakhawat Hossain.

Rokeya was born in a small village called Pairaband, now in Bangladesh. Her father was a wealthy but conservative zamindar. He encouraged his sons to study but his daughters were kept in strict purdah. They were hidden even from visiting females, and forbidden from learning anything other than Arabic. It was felt that anything else would contaminate girls' minds.

Rokeya and her sister, Karimunnesa, however, were determined to learn Bengali and English. And so, Rokeya observed while Karimunnesa quietly scratched the Bengali alphabet on the ground in the courtyard. They waited till everyone had gone to sleep before sneaking English lessons from their obliging brothers! The two sisters managed to learn five languages — Arabic, Persian, Bengali, Urdu and English. They encouraged each other to write. Karimunnesa wrote poetry and Rokeya began to write essays in English and Bengali.

But Karimunnesa's poetry was discovered by disapproving family members and she was packed off to her grandparents. By 16 she was married, never to write anything more. Rokeya was traumatised by the waste of her sister's talent, and more determined than ever to fight customs to continue her own learning.

She married Syed Sakhawat Hossain, a liberal and well educated man about 20 years older than her. They moved to Bhagalpur, Bihar, where he was the district magistrate. He was proud of Rokeya's learning and encouraged her literary interests. So Rokeya read all the books she could get, in all the languages she knew. And the more she read, the more she realised how much her Bengali Muslim sisters were losing out by not being allowed an education.

"Then she screwed a couple of seats onto a square piece of plank. To this plank she attached two smooth and well-polished balls. When I asked her what the balls were for, she said they were hydrogen balls and they were used to overcome the force of gravity ... She then fastened to the air-car two wing-like blades, which, she said, were worked by electricity. After we were comfortably seated she touched a knob and the blades began to whirl, moving faster and faster every moment. At first we were raised to the height of about six or seven feet and then off we flew..."
From *Sultana's Dream*

"It is surprising that such a depiction [*Sultana's Dream*] came from the pen of a young Muslim woman from colonial Bengal..."
Tahmima Anam, Bangladeshi novelist, 2011

One day, when Sakhawat came back from a long official tour, Rokeya surprised him with her very first English story, *Sultana's Dream*. He was so impressed that he persuaded Rokeya to have it published. The story seems a simple satire where gender roles are reversed in a utopian world, and marvellous scientific inventions are devised by clever women. But there is a hidden message — women need to be empowered for a better world.

Rokeya's pen now became her voice. Using her brilliant mind, she began to write and publish essays and articles in Bengali. She questioned the social order that denied women basic rights. To all who argued that women were physically weak and intellectually inferior, she had this to say: Women and men are made equal by god. Over the centuries, women steadily had all their rights taken away from them until they reached a point where they were subordinate to men. Her message to women who were made to feel inferior was, "Jago go, bhogin! (Wake up, sisters!)" She wanted them to rise, to stop accepting the role of slaves. And in Rokeya's view, education was the key to this awakening.

Sadly, Sakhawat died a few years later. Knowing what Rokeya wanted more than anything else, he left her a substantial amount of money to be used for women's education. Rokeya started a school for Muslim girls in Bhagalpur and then, in 1911, she opened the Sakhawat Memorial Girls' School in Kolkata. There were only eight admissions.

Conservative Muslim society was shocked at the thought of their daughters being asked to step out of the house. Some were angry and hostile, others were confused. Rokeya patiently went from house to house persuading people of the benefits of having educated daughters — in future, as wives and mothers they would make a strong community. She even came up with a 'purdah horse carriage' so no one would see the girls while going to school! She made sure her girls learnt not just home economics and fine arts but science and physical education, so they could be strong in mind and body. The school was based on Indian rather than Western traditions, giving the girls a grounding in their own culture. In four years, the number of students went up to 84.

The Sakhawat Memorial Girls' School still runs today, a tribute to its courageous founder who herself never had the chance to go to school.

"[We] should open the door to our development with our own hands. Unless we worry about ourselves, no one else is going to worry for us … So I say … all of you together, go forward in the name of freedom … Let us do all that has to be done to gain equality with men."
Begum Rokeya

"…Rokeya … displayed an unwavering faith in the promise of the liberated feminine. It was that belief which lent her the courage to interrogate the politics of the nineteenth and early twentieth century subcontinental (Muslim) patriarchy and fight for women's right to life and freedom."
Nabanipa Bhattacharjee, sociologist

SHE DARED TO DREAM

1880

Born on 9 December in Pairaband village, Rangpur, in Bengal (now Bangladesh), into a well-off but orthodox Muslim family. Is allowed to learn only Arabic to be able to read the Quran, but picks up Persian and Urdu, and learns Bengali and English with the help of her brothers.

1896

At 16 is married to 38-year-old Syed Sakhawat Hossain, who is Western educated and progressive minded. He encourages Rokeya to learn, read and write.

1900s

In 1902, adopts Bengali for her literary works and launches her career, which spans 30 years, with her first essay in Bengali titled *Pipasha* ('Thirst').

Starts writing for the *Nabanoor* magazine in 1903 under the name of Mrs R. S. Hossain. Also begins to contribute to *Nabaprabha, Mahila, Saogat, Mohammedi* and other magazines.

Writes *Sultana's Dream*, her first and only story in English, and one of the earliest works of science fiction in India. It is published in 1905 in *The Indian Ladies' Magazine*, Chennai, the first Indian magazine in English to be established and edited by an Indian woman — Kamala Satthianadhan — and written by and for women.

After her husband's death in 1909, she starts a school for Muslim girls in Bhagalpur — with 5 students and 2 benches!

1910s

Has to move to Kolkata in 1910. Sets up the English medium Sakhawat Memorial Girls' School with 8 students. Now run by the West Bengal government the school is considered one of the best in the area.

বেগম রোকেয়া বিশ্ববিদ্যালয়, রংপুর

জ্ঞানই শক্তি

Begum Rokeya University, Rangpur

Trains herself to teach and to administer. The curriculum she plans is much ahead of the times, and includes physical exercise and vocational programmes.

Comes up with the term 'manoshik dashotto', meaning mental slavery, identifying it as the reason for the subjugation of women, Muslims in particular, the antidote to which is education and learning.

Founds the Anjuman-e-Khawateen-e-Islam (Muslim Women's Society) in 1913 — a pioneering organisation that provides vocational training and literacy classes for destitute women, and helps poor Muslim women with financial support. Seen as an important milestone of the feminist movement in the region and the world.

Due to her persistent efforts, in 1919 the government sets up the Muslim Women's Training School in Kolkata to train teachers.

1926

Is invited to chair the Bengal Women's Educational Conference, where she says: "Although I am grateful to you for the respect ... I am forced to say that you have not made the right choice. I have been locked up in the socially oppressive iron casket of 'porda' for all my life. I have not been able to mix very well with people — as a matter of fact, I do not even know what is expected of a chairperson!"

1932

After putting the finishing touches the night before on 'Narir Odhikar', an article on women's rights, she dies in Kolkata on 9 December — which is also her birth date, and now celebrated as Rokeya Day in Bangladesh.

Her undiluted passion for the social uplift of women earned praise and cooperation from other women luminaries of her time, such as Sarojini Naidu, Queen Sultan Jahan of Bhopal, Lady Chelmsford and Lady Carmichael. In Bangladesh, she is seen as perhaps their first feminist.

சுப்பிரமணிய பாரதி

SUBRAMANIA BHARATI

1882–1921

In the early, turbulent days of the
freedom movement, nationalistic newspapers
added a sharp edge to the fight against the colonial state.
Their courageous proprietors risked persecution and imprisonment.
The mercurial young Subramania Bharati cut his teeth on this
radical journalism. But his fiery writing really exploded in his
poetry and songs, which spoke for freedom, justice and
a progressive India. And to Tamil, a language rich with two
millennia of history, he gave an original contemporary
voice that still resonates with the common people.

SUBRAMANIA BHARATI WOULD HAVE been amused to know that there were just 11 people at his funeral. In life, the writer had been fearless, outspoken and never afraid to question injustice. So, it was only natural that by the time he died, he had annoyed quite a few people — the British colonial government, as well as many traditionalists who found him just a bit too radical.

He was only 39 years old at the time. His works of prose and poetry lay scattered — uncollected and unpublished. The young family he left behind was virtually penniless. And yet, just a few years later, he was so famous that every schoolchild could identify the picture of the turbaned face with the bristling moustache and fiery eyes. People squabbled so much over the rights to use and publish his works that finally the government of Tamil Nadu bought the copyright to all of it and made it freely available! His writing now belonged to the nation.

This sudden change in fortune would not have surprised anyone who knew him as a young boy. By the age of seven, the prodigy was already dazzling his friends and teachers in his hometown Ettayapuram in Tamil Nadu, with his improvised verse and poetry. At 11, he was confident enough to have discussions on Tamil literature with scholars. The maharaja of Ettayapuram was impressed and gave him the title of 'Bharati' — 'one blessed by Saraswati', the goddess of learning.

Subramania's life seemed to gallop along at a very fast trot. By the time he was 16, he had lost both parents and was married to seven-year-old Chellamma. He went to live with an aunt in Varanasi to continue his education, and it is here that he was exposed to a whole new world of cultural and political ideas. When he returned to Ettayapuram, he was fluent in English, Sanskrit and Urdu. He now sported the trademark turban and beard.

Bharatiar, as he is best known, had a flair for language that landed him a job as a sub-editor of the first Tamil daily newspaper, *Swadesamitran*, and launched his career as a journalist. Plunging headlong into political activity, he travelled all over India, attending Congress meetings and engaging with leaders and thinkers of the time. Bal Gangadhar Tilak's call for direct and sometimes militant action against British rule appealed to the firebrand in him. He became one of the Extremists in the Congress party, and soon the editor of *India*, their weekly paper,

"Do you argue, that things ancient ought, on that account, to be true and noble?"
Subramania Bharati

"Poet Bharati ... has kindled the souls of men and women by the million to a more passionate love of freedom, and a richer dedication to the service of the country."
Sarojini Naidu, Independence leader and poet

"For Bharati, nationalism could never mean a turning inward, a focus on national interest in the narrow sense, to the exclusion of the world at large."
Mira T. Sundara Rajan, Subramania Bharati's granddaughter, 2017

writing fiery editorials. He was among the first in the country to introduce political cartoons on the front page, which took quiet digs at the British.

One day, after a particularly hard-hitting cartoon, the owner of *India* was arrested. Bharatiar fled to neighbouring French-ruled Puducherry — taking the press along with him! For a while, copies of *India* were smuggled across the Puducherry border until the British banned the paper altogether.

But Bharatiar had another ace up his sleeve: poetry.

Although he had a vast knowledge of classical Tamil language and literature, he decided to use words and rhythms that were easily understood. He churned out prose, poetry, free verse, songs, and even haiku. His themes were modern, with humour and satire. It was a whole new style of contemporary Tamil literature.

He wrote on topics closest to his heart as a political journalist — freedom from a foreign power, suffering of a colonised people, sacrifices of freedom fighters. He wrote songs to inspire children, and stories in which he described India's great physical and spiritual beauty and his love of Tamil culture. He translated world literature so Indians could view themselves in relation to the rest of the world.

But he also criticised the failings of Indian society — caste divisions, ignorance, and regressive social traditions. He believed that the struggle for independence was meaningless without equality between men and women. To him, dividing people on the basis of caste was a sin.

Unfortunately, outspoken writers like him were on the British watchlist. Back in Chennai after his ten-year exile, all his efforts to get his works published failed. He slipped deep into poverty. After a bizarre accident involving a temple elephant, Bharatiar fell seriously ill and did not recover.

Soon after, the Independence movement gathered steam. The publishing industry expanded, and newspapers and books took his works outside the small circle in Tamil Nadu. Bharatiar's words and lyrics captured the imagination of patriots all over India. As films and gramophone records became popular, his poems turned into slogans, and his songs rang through cinema halls... As he had hoped, his words had stirred fellow Indians to fight for freedom and justice.

"When you are young, Bharati fires your imagination. His language, suffused with idealism, remains inspiring for anyone who is unhappy with the status quo. And that Bharati stays with you for life..."

"Contemporary Tamil works are filled with allusions to his writings. Bharati is not history. Numerous writers have taken their pen names with 'Bharati' as suffix. If one wanted to name a new journal or find an inspiring motto to adorn the banner, you could no better than resort to his lines."

A. R. Venkatachalapathy, historian and Tamil writer, 2018

Swadesamitran

Without social
reform our
political reform is
a dream,
a myth, for social
slaves can never
really understand
political liberty.

C. Subramania Bharati

SONGS OF FREEDOM

1882

C. Subramania is born on 11 December in Ettayapuram, Tirunelveli District, Tamil Nadu.

1893

The maharaja of Ettayapuram recognises his poetic brilliance. Is given the title of 'Bharati'.

1897

Marries Chellamma, who is the inspiration behind his romantic poems.

1898

Devastated by the death of his father, he goes to live with his aunt in Varanasi. There he is exposed to the national movement.

1902

Invited by the maharaja of Ettayayapuram to work in his samastana, or court.

1904

Drawn to journalism and the need to be aware of the wider world. Joins as sub-editor of *Swadesamitran*, the first Tamil daily newspaper, with strong connections to the Indian National Congress (INC).

1906

Alongside *Swadesamitran*, becomes editor of *Chakravartini*, a magazine for women. Writes a kural (couplet) for the header that says: "With more knowledge for women, womanhood becomes great; when this happens, the country becomes great."

Attends the Kolkata session of INC headed by Dadabhai Naoroji. The demand for Swaraj and boycott of British goods is adopted. Meets Sister Nivedita, disciple of Swami Vivekananda — is a big influence on Bharatiar's ideas for women's rights and freedom.

1907

Drops both earlier magazines to become editor of the Tamil weekly, *India*, started by patriots of the freedom struggle, the Mandayam family. It takes the slogan of the French Revolution as its motto: Liberty, Equality, Fraternity.

Is a pioneer of column writing in Tamil and, among non-English papers, of carrying political cartoons on the front page.

Bharatiar also brings out an English newspaper for the youth, *Bala Bharata*.

Three of his national poems are first published as a booklet: *Vande Mataram*, *Nattu Vanakkam* and *Engal Nadu*.

Attends the historic Surat Congress where he meets Lala Lajpat Rai, Bal Gangadhar Tilak and Bipin Chandra Pal. Joins the Lal-Bal-Pal Extremists group.

1908

Crackdown on *India*. Bharati escapes to Puducherry and continues to publish several papers from there.

His ten years in self-exile turn out to be his most productive writing years. Is also in close contact with revolutionaries Aurobindo Ghosh and V. V. S. Iyer.

1913

To protest against the caste system, he performs a 'sacred thread' ceremony for a Dalit boy.

1918

Leaves Puducherry. Is arrested and imprisoned in Cuddalore for 20 days. Prison affects his health.

1919

Meets Mahatma Gandhi briefly in Chennai.

1920

Resumes work with *Swadesamitran.*

His Muslim friends invite him to speak at a meeting. Bharati composes a song on Allah, later published in his work *The Greatness of Islam.*

1921

Injured by a temple elephant. Gives his last speech at the Karungalpalayam Library in Erode a few days later, on the immortality of man. Dies soon after on 11 September.

1949

The Tamil Nadu government buys copyright to all his works — compensating his family — and makes them available to everyone.

Mahakavi Bharatiar's poems run to about 600 pages. As part of his deep imprint on Tamil are three words that he coined: pudmai pen ('new woman'), puratchi ('revolution') and poduvudamai ('communism').

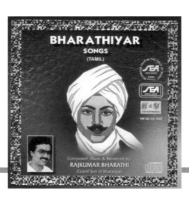

சி. வி. ராமன்

C. V. RAMAN

1888–1970

It was the Age of Science.
The origin of humankind, atomic theory,
electromagnetic waves... these were matters hotly discussed.
In the science centres of the West, a race was on for funding,
revamped education and new research establishments. Far away from
these dramatic developments, C. V. Raman worked with minimal
facilities. But he showed how a profound curiosity about the world
around, self-belief, and some genius, could go a long
way – right up to the Nobel Prize! With scientists
still analysing the magnitude of his work, he paved
the way for Indian science in the world.

"WHY IS THE sea blue?"

Chandrasekhara Venkata Raman leaned over the railings of the SS Narkunda, gazing in wonder at the deep blue of the Mediterranean Sea. It was 1921, and the professor of physics from Calcutta University was on his way back from a conference in England. That simple question led to a series of experiments and a discovery so path-breaking that it eventually won him the Nobel Prize.

C. V. Raman was the classic child genius. His father was a lecturer in maths and physics, and from a young age Raman read his way through a wide variety of books on science and astronomy. He also loved English literature and music. By 19, he was done with both bachelor's and master's degrees, topping his class, and winning plenty of distinctions and gold medals along the way. Confused college lecturers were known to have turned the small-made Raman out of class, taking him for a young boy who had wandered in there by mistake!

Since there were few job opportunities in science in those days, he joined the Financial Civil Service as an accountant and moved to Kolkata. But his heart lay in physics and he continued to conduct experiments with rudimentary equipment at home. One day, while commuting to work on a tram, he saw a sign that read 'Indian Association for the Cultivation of Science'. Legend has it that Raman jumped out of the moving tram and ran inside the building!

He began to work in the IACS labs after work, and was soon writing and publishing scientific papers on acoustics and optics which were being read and appreciated by an international audience. He quit his accountant's job when he was offered the Palit Chair of Physics at Calcutta University. Shortly after his appointment, he was sent to England to attend the Congress of Universities of the British Empire. It was a voyage that led to his most remarkable discovery.

At the time he was wondering about the deep blue of the ocean, some scientists had already concluded that the colour was due to the reflection of the sky. But Raman had an idea of his own. He believed it might have something to do with the interaction of light with water. He spent the rest of the journey back to India conducting experiments with some basic equipment he had carried with him.

"Young friends, I want you to realise that the spirit of science is not in finding short and quick answers. The spirit of science is to delve deeper and deeper ... One thing leads to another. That is the essence of science. You must go where it leads you. The moment you raise a question another question arises, then another ... Ultimately you find you have to travel the whole field of science to get the answer for why the sky is blue."

C. V. Raman in his talk to children, 'Why the Sky is Blue', 1968

When the ship finally berthed in Mumbai, he went straight to the harbour post office and mailed his findings in a letter to the journal *Nature*! Raman had come to the conclusion that the colour of the sea was not a reflection of the sky at all, but due to the way light was scattered by water molecules.

In Kolkata, Raman and his students went full tilt into researching light scattering. The breakthrough came in 1928. He was able to conclude that when you shoot a beam of light on an object, a very small part of the light interacts with the atoms of that object and scatters light in a unique pattern or spectrum. The light that then emerges is of a different colour and depends on the nature of the molecules in the object. These emerging colours are very tiny and difficult to detect.

This came to be known as The Raman Effect.

The discovery took the scientific world by storm. It was certainly important for the new study of quantum physics — the study of things at the micro level. But today scientists are discovering even more important roles for the Raman Effect in the field of chemistry. Every substance, when light is shone on it, has its own Raman pattern — as unique as a fingerprint. Scanning a substance reveals its chemical composition instantly, without having to go through complicated or time-consuming lab tests. With new laser technology, 'Raman scanners' are now being used to detect everything from illegal drugs at airports to cancer cells in the brain. Scientists are in the process of building up databases of Raman patterns for all materials.

He was showered with awards, finally winning the 1930 Nobel Prize. India was still under colonial rule with limited access to international research and publications. And now an Indian, who had done all his research in India, had won the Nobel!

Inclined to be quick tempered with adults, Raman was very patient with children. He could explain complicated scientific principles to them in ways that they enjoyed and understood. His popular science talks were more like performances, full of logic and humour. One such lecture, 'Why the Sky is Blue', is legendary.

Raman believed that the scientific spirit could be developed by simply being curious about everyday life. He often said, "Ask the right questions and nature will open the door to her secrets." After all, that is what he had done.

"Raman's enduring legacy is in evidence on the cover of the latest *Science Translational Medicine*, a prestigious journal ...
[A few days ago] a team of scientists from Harvard University and the University of Michigan revealed a sophisticated new technique that uses mild lasers to create a colour-coded map of cancerous cells in the brain, holding out hope of more accurate surgery on deadly tumours. Neurosurgeon Daniel Orringer and his colleagues use a greatly amped version of the Raman effect ...
'The great discoveries of C. V. Raman are at the core of SRS [Stimulated Raman Scattering] microscopy,' said Orringer. 'Without his work, SRS microscopy would not be possible.'"

Samar Halarnkar, journalist, 2013

THE RAMAN EFFECT

1930

Look at the resplendent colours
on the soap bubbles!
Why is the sea blue?
What makes diamond glitter!
Ask the right questions, and
nature will open the doors to
her secrets!

THE RAMAN EFFECT

1888

Born in Tiruchirapalli, Tamilnadu, on 7 November, to a family that is scholarly if not very well off.

1890s

Grows up in Visakhapatnam, Andhra Pradesh. Is always interested in science and reading ahead of his age.

Likes to explain science and scientific things to his younger siblings.

1900s

Gets a bachelor's degree in 1904 from Presidency College, Chennai. Wins gold medals in physics and English. His British professors encourage him to go to England to study, but his doctor advises him not to on account of his fragile health.

In 1906, his first academic paper on the behaviour of light appears in the prestigious *Philosophical Magazine* of London. After a second article in the magazine, gets a letter from Nobel physicist Lord Rayleigh, who addresses him as "Professor Raman", not realising he's a teenaged student!

Completes his master's in physics in 1907 with the highest distinction. Tops the Financial Civil Service exam (FCS). Joins the Indian Finance Department as the assistant accountant general in Kolkata.

Spends all his free time at the Indian Association for Cultivation of Science (IACS). Researches acoustics of Indian musical instruments — how the sound and notes of the tabla and mridangam are produced.

1910s

In 1917, is appointed Palit Professor of Physics at the University of Calcutta by Sir Ashutosh Mookerjee. For the first time, the post is given to someone who has never studied abroad.

Becomes Honorary Secretary of IACS in 1919, a post he holds till 1933.

1920s

Attends a conference at Oxford in 1921. On the return voyage by ship, is struck by the colour of the Mediterranean Sea, he re-examines Rayleigh's theory about the sea reflecting the sky.

Starts the *Indian Journal of Physics* in 1926, of which he is the first editor.

On 28 February 1927, Raman and his team, including K. S. Krishnan, discover the phenomenon of light scattering. The German physicist Peter Pringsheim later coins the term 'Der Raman Effekt' or 'The Raman Effect'. Today we celebrate the date as National Science Day.

Presents his theory at a meeting of the South Indian Science Association in Bengaluru in 1928. Copies of his speech are sent to scientists all over the world.

Made a Knight of the British Empire in 1929.

1930s

In 1930, wins the Nobel Prize for Physics — the first Asian to be awarded the Nobel in any field of science, and the only scientist educated, trained and working in India to do so. He is so sure that he will win it that he books his ticket to Sweden four months before the announcement!

Becomes Director, Indian Institute of Science (IISc), Bengaluru, in 1933 — the first Indian to hold this post.

1940s

Becomes India's first National Professor in 1947.

In 1948, retires from IISc.

Establishes the Raman Research Institute (RRI) in Bengaluru in 1949, for conducting scientific research in different fields of physics. Works there till the end.

1954

Awarded the Bharat Ratna.

1970

Dies in Bengaluru. Two days before that he tells one of his former students, "Do not allow the journals of the academy [RRI] to die, for they are the sensitive indicators of the quality of science being done in the country and whether science is taking root in it or not."

जवाहरलाल नेहरू

JAWAHARLAL NEHRU

1889–1964

India stood at a crossroads.

The euphoria of Independence lay behind,
ahead was the challenge of building a new nation. Staring
back was a grim reality – the festering wounds of Partition,
poverty, hunger, and a vast, diverse population. For Nehru
as the prime minister, it was a mammoth task. Institutions,
industries and infrastructure were certainly needed, but he
was clear about where he wanted to begin. His first focus
was on a Constitution that would lay a strong foundation
for democracy, giving power to the people.
It was his blueprint for free India.

TAKE A LOOK at these addresses.

Anand Bhawan, Allahabad. Harrow School, London. Trinity College, Cambridge. Inner Temple, Inns of Court, London. Lucknow Jail. Dehradun Jail. Naini Central Prison. Teen Murti Bhavan, Delhi... Quite an assortment, you will agree. And somehow symbolic of the life led by India's first prime minister, Jawaharlal Nehru.

He grew up in a sprawling home called Anand Bhawan in Allahabad, the son of a wealthy lawyer. His education was a privileged mix of private tutors, and an elite school and university in England. But it was also one where, thanks to his father Motilal Nehru's political activity, he engaged in intellectual and political discussion at home. There were books everywhere on philosophy, history and literature which he devoured, strongly affected by stories of inequality, injustice, blind faith and oppression. The young bookworm even dreamt of leading his own nation to freedom like the swashbuckling Italian general, Garibaldi.

In 1912, Nehru returned to India armed with his law degree from England, and discovered that he was not really that interested in law after all! What really drew him was politics. He joined the Congress and quickly became a close confidante and protégé of Mahatma Gandhi. Being brilliant and articulate, Nehru was able to communicate the aims of the Congress party to the elite as well as the masses. He was sent to jail nine times — almost nine years of his life were spent in prison! Unfazed, he spent his time with his old friends — books! — reading up to 20 in a month. He wrote some himself, which are still popular for their impeccable research, language and vision.

He also spent time thinking about the issues that India would face as it went forward to freedom. Which was just as well, because when Independence came in 1947, Nehru was appointed prime minister.

There was no hiding the fact that things did not look too good. Two centuries of colonial rule had reduced a once rich nation to poverty. Almost a million people had died during Partition. Over ten million refugees had to be resettled. Food and funds were in short supply. There were regional, ethnic and religious divisions. More than 500 princely states had still not agreed to join India. Literacy levels were as low as 14 per cent. And within months, Mahatma Gandhi was assassinated.

"A moment comes, which comes but rarely in history, when we step out from the old to the new, when an age ends, and when the soul of a nation, long suppressed, finds utterance."
Jawaharlal Nehru

"He himself was such a convinced democrat, profoundly wary of the risks of autocracy, that, at the crest of his rise, he authored an anonymous article warning Indians of the dangers of giving dictatorial temptations to Jawaharlal Nehru. 'He must be checked,' he wrote of himself. 'We want no Caesars.'"
Shashi Tharoor, writer and politician, 2018

It was as if Nehru had been training for the challenge all his life. He came into the job with a clear vision for the country that he and his fellow freedom fighters had fought and sacrificed for. The foundation of this was democracy. And the first task was to write a Constitution that would guarantee every Indian justice, equality and freedom of thought. India's culture had been built over centuries by people with their own distinct identities — each of them deserved their place in the new India.

With the help of distinguished colleagues, Nehru was able to present one of the finest Constitutions in the world. He insisted on Universal Adult Franchise — one vote per adult. There were plenty who insisted that the people were too poor, too illiterate to vote. He proved the doubters wrong. He travelled more than 40,000 km, addressing over 35 million people, explaining the system to them. The 1952 general elections were the largest of its kind in the world, with 173 million first-time voters.

Nehru cut a dashing figure with his sherwani, rose in his buttonhole and distinctive white cap. He was wildly popular among the common people who voted him into power over almost 18 years. He could well have turned arrogant or dictatorial. As it was, many other newly liberated colonies were headed rapidly towards dictatorships. Instead, he was determined to make democracy work. He showed respect for parliament, courtesy to the opposition, and deference to the president. He also kept up a stream of letters to chief ministers of states asking for feedback on his policies.

To cope with the problems of poverty and inequality, Nehru decided that important heavy industries and natural resources would be state regulated. A science enthusiast, he also encouraged homegrown scientific research, setting up centres of design, management and engineering to give India a talented pool of technical people. Later there was some criticism of this model. But even the critics have to agree that today, thanks to those policies, India has a sound industrial and technical advantage in the world. Internationally, he carved out a place for India through the Non-Aligned Movement. The message went out that, though poor and struggling, India was free to take its own decisions.

Today's independent, democratic, secular and multicultural India can definitely thank that little boy curled up in some corner of his father's mansion, with his nose buried in a book.

"Nehru instinctively understood the utility of a constitutional democracy for a people with disparate identities; India was also lucky to have a generation of other gifted leaders like B.R. Ambedkar, Vallabhbhai Patel, Maulana Azad and C. Rajagopalachari and together they crafted a political framework for Indians to coexist and evolve a shared imagination of the nation while preserving specific identities."

"Gandhi is understood to be a sage but Nehru was no less a counsellor to India, constantly drawing attention to the principles and direction of its politics and society. He inspired, he cajoled, he rebuked. He also failed. He worked tirelessly."

Sushil Aaron, journalist, 2018

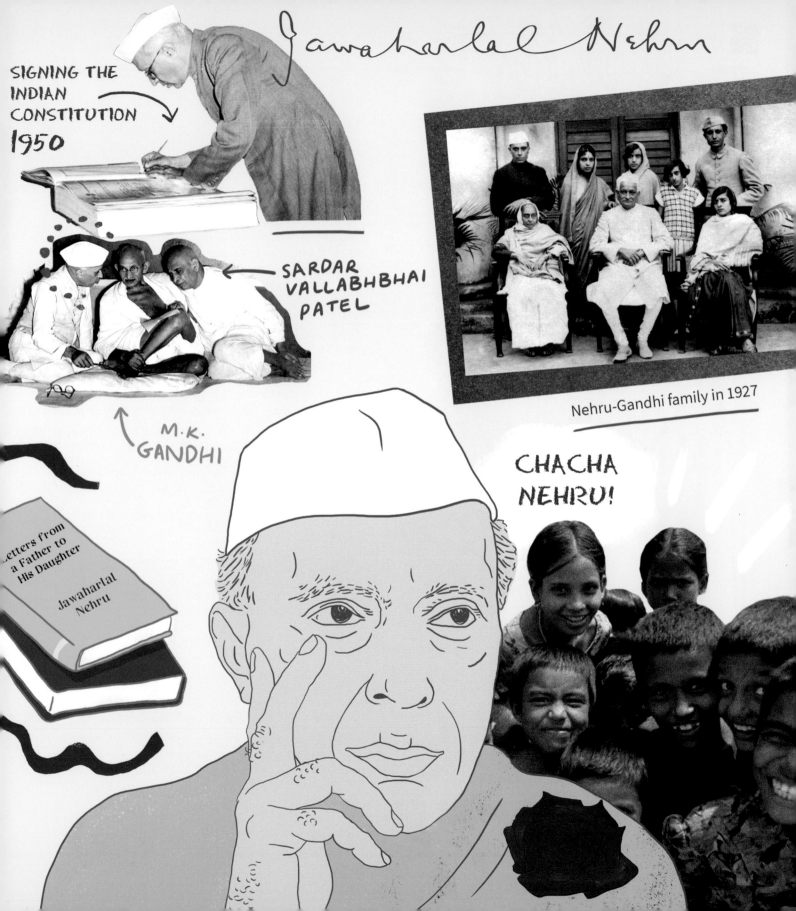

Jawaharlal Nehru

SIGNING THE INDIAN CONSTITUTION 1950

SARDAR VALLABHBHAI PATEL

M·K· GANDHI

Letters from a Father to His Daughter

Jawaharlal Nehru

Nehru-Gandhi family in 1927

CHACHA NEHRU!

BUILDING INDIA

1889

Born into a Kashmiri family in Allahabad on
14 November, now celebrated as Children's Day.

1905

After home-schooling for some years, goes to Harrow
School, England. Continues on to Trinity College,
Cambridge, and then to study law at the Inner Temple.

1910s

Returns to India in 1912, joins the Allahabad High Court.
Attends a session of the Indian National Congress (INC) at
Patna, and starts working for the party.

Meets Gandhi for the first time at a joint INC and Muslim
League session in Lucknow in 1916, where Hindu-Muslim
unity is agreed upon. Talks for this Lucknow Pact had begun
earlier at Anand Bhawan, the Nehru house in Allahalbad.

Is influenced by Annie Besant and joins the Home Rule
League in 1917, of which he later becomes the secretary.

Joins Gandhi in protest against the Jallianwala Bagh
massacre in 1919.

1920s–1930s

Is actively involved in all the major movements towards
freedom, and imprisoned several times.

Takes India's cause to the world. In 1927, represents India
in the League against Imperialism at the Congress of
Oppressed Nationalities in Brussels.

At INC's Lahore session in 1929 drafts the Purna Swaraj
declaration for complete self-rule and independence, which
says, "We believe that it is the inalienable right of the Indian
people, as of any other people, to have freedom and to
enjoy the fruits of their toil…" Is elected president of INC,
and hoists the tricolour flag of India for the first time.

Drafts the Fundamental Rights and Economic Policy in 1929–31, which is ratified by the Karachi session of the Congress headed by Vallabhbhai Patel.

Goes to Europe in 1936 to be with his ailing wife. His earlier interest in socialism and Marxism grows.

1940s

An interim government is formed in 1946, with Nehru as vice-president of the Viceroy's Executive Council.

The run up to freedom sees the Muslim League headed by Muhammad Ali Jinnah insisting on a separate nation. Nehru, Patel and Jinnah all reject Gandhi's idea of Jinnah as prime minister of an undivided India. Nehru also rejects Jinnah's idea of a loosely federal structure for India, saying a strong centre is important. Partition follows, and riots.

On the midnight of 14–15 August 1947, delivers his iconic 'Tryst with Destiny' speech in parliament as the prime minister of independent India.

Keen that India has cutting-edge scientific capacity. In 1948, sets up the Atomic Energy Commission headed by Homi Bhabha, who is to report only to him.

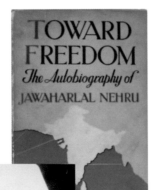

1950s

In 1950, becomes chairman of the National Planning Commission. Launches the First Five-Year Plan for India's development focusing on agriculture and industry.

First general elections are held in 1951–52. Nehru becomes the elected prime minister of India, and is also the foreign minister.

In 1953, appoints a commission to reorganise states along linguistic lines.

Signs the Panchsheel agreement with China in 1954, which establishes five guiding principles of peaceful coexistence.

In 1955, is a key initiator of a conference in Bandung, Indonesia, for talks on a Non-Aligned Movement among newly independent Asian and African nations.

Awarded the Bharat Ratna in 1955.

Congress wins a huge victory again in the 1957 elections.

1960s

Takes a moral stand against the divisions of the Cold War. In 1961, leads an alliance of developing countries to stay neutral and form the Non-Aligned Movement.

Congress wins the 1962 elections too, but with a reduced majority.

The Chinese invade the northeast in 1962, after showing signs of friendship. Many blame Nehru for India's losses.

Feels terribly betrayed by the Chinese, and unhappy about the war. His health deteriorates and he passes away in 1964.

बाबासाहेब आंबेडकर

BABASAHEB AMBEDKAR

1891–1956

Touchable, Untouchable.
The words defined his life. They were an age-old caste
decree that heaped insensitive humiliation on him and everyone in his
community. But it could not stop Bhimrao Ambedkar from reaching
unprecedented heights. And finally, the country reached out to his
brilliance, choosing him to guide the creation of new India's
Constitution. This was his chance to right centuries of wrong meted
out to Dalits, the 'broken' – the Untouchables. For years he had been
the voice of these voiceless millions. Now he made them equal
by law. Today, "Jai Bhim!" is the clarion call of the
anti-caste Ambedkarite movement.

IMAGINE THIS LITTLE BOY going to school. He is made to sit on a gunny sack at the back of the classroom. The teacher will not touch his notebook, so the boy has to hold it up to show his work. He is not permitted to touch the water tap. If he needs water, the school peon is summoned to turn it on. If the peon happens to be on holiday, the boy goes thirsty.

What did the boy do to deserve such cruel treatment? He was simply born into a certain caste that others called Untouchable.

This is the searing story of the early life of Bhimrao Ramji Ambavadekar — later Ambedkar — also known as Babasaheb. He was born in a family of Mahars, a caste on the lowest rungs of society that, according to their religious belief, upper caste Hindus saw as 'unclean' and 'polluting'. With the coming of the East India Company, many of them, like Bhimrao's father, found a way out of this miserable existence by joining the army. Schools would not take in their children. When they did, unable to bear the nasty treatment, most children dropped out.

In Bhimrao's case, the teacher could not turn him away since it was a government-funded school. It was soon obvious that the boy was not just exceptionally gifted but equally determined to get an education. He worked hard, often waking up at two in the morning to study. He won scholarships to stellar institutions, eventually becoming one of the most highly educated Indians of his time with two doctorates and a bar-at-law from distinguished universities abroad!

When he left India he found something surprising. He realised he was expected to sit at the same table as everyone else, and there was no fuss about which plate he was using or which glass he had drunk from. In this atmosphere of equality, he blossomed. He absorbed the teachings of eminent scholars of economics, political science, history and philosophy. He developed new skills in analysis and critical thinking. He honed his writing abilities and read widely, building up a library of more than 2000 books. Exposure to new cultures enabled him to look at his own country with fresh eyes. He changed.

But on his return to India, Ambedkar realised that his country had not.

His well-wisher, the maharaja of Baroda, gave him a prestigious job. But within months, he was forced to quit because he could not find a place to live. No landlord would rent out to a so-called Untouchable! The humiliation cut deep.

"One day ... the class teacher called upon Bhim to come to the blackboard to solve an example ... [T]here was an uproar in the class. The caste Hindu children used to keep their tiffin-boxes behind the blackboard. Since they feared that their food would be polluted by Bhim's presence near the board, they dashed to the blackboard and hurled their tiffin-boxes aside before Bhim could reach and touch the blackboard."

Dhananjay Keer in *Dr Ambedkar: Life and Mission*

"The newspapers used to publish a lot about Gandhi, Jawarharlal Nehru, Abul Kalam Azad, Subhash Chandra Bose ... We knew these leaders belonged to the upper castes ... I used to wonder, 'Who is our leader?' I asked Abba this, and he replied, 'Ummedkar, the one who brings hope,' which is how Abba saw Babasaheb Ambedkar."

Bhagwan Das, Dalit historian, in *Ambedkar: The Attendant Details*

Ambedkar knew something drastic would have to be done for his countrymen to overcome their prejudices.

He moved to Mumbai and took up various jobs as tutor, accountant, lecturer and lawyer. He turned his brilliantly trained mind to find a voice for the most downtrodden and oppressed, through a blitz of writing, publishing and activism. He formed welfare organisations and led agitations. He started a weekly called *Mooknayak* ('Leader of the Voiceless'), calling for radical changes in Hindu society and an end to caste oppression. He represented the Depressed Classes, the so-called lower castes, at all three Round Table Conferences in London. These views brought him into conflict with many powerful people of the day. Including Mahatma Gandhi.

Gandhi thought that Hindus could overcome caste taboos with love, and offered to be a representative of the Untouchables whom he called Harijans, 'children of god'. Ambedkar wanted a complete break from Hinduism because he did not think Hindus could change their deeply ingrained beliefs. He even publicly burnt copies of *Manusmriti*, the highly unequal laws of Manu that ruled Hindu society.

His ideas clashed with the ideals of the Congress party too. While freedom from colonial rule was important, felt Ambedkar, it was of no value when so many Indians lived in social and economic conditions that were less than human. He wanted practical moves to first set right the injustices of Indian society.

Despite these differences, no one could afford to ignore the sheer intellectual ability of Ambedkar. When Independence came, he was made the law minister and the chairman of the Drafting Committee for the new Constitution.

After months of intense debate and several revisions, the Constitution of India was finalised, and adopted in January 1950. It bore the stamp of Ambedkar's great intelligence and keen understanding of India's political and economic problems. Every individual, male or female, was made a free and equal citizen of India. Untouchability was abolished! Those who had been oppressed for thousands of years found hope and a fair chance to find their feet through reservations in jobs and education.

Ambedkar had forced his country to acknowledge the shame of social injustice.

"The huge grounds of Gogate College in Ratnagiri were soon overrun by people who poured in from everywhere. The ground was packed to capacity ... announcements were being made. Then the notes of 'Budhdham Saranam Gachchhami (I seek refuge in the Buddha)' came floating down to us and we joined our singing voices with the singing crowd."

Urmila Pawar, Dalit feminist writer, on her conversion to Buddhism, influenced by Ambedkar

"Anti-caste leaders have been raising issues faced by Bahujan students in campuses. But that was never looked at as an issue of 'national importance'. It took a Dalit student's death for everyone to wake up to the crisis ... But this political mileage can be sustained only if a clear roadmap is developed with the Bahujans leading the way ... possible only if Ambedkar's values of constitutional democracy are treated as the core principle of any political movement."

Sukanya Shantha, journalist, 2019

March to Mahad

CHAIRMAN,
Drafting Committee of
the Indian Constitution

THE
CONSTITUTION OF INDIA

WE, THE PEOPLE OF INDIA, having solemnly
resolved to constitute India into a SOVEREIGN DEMO-
CRATIC REPUBLIC and to secure to all its citizens:
  JUSTICE, social, economic and political;
  LIBERTY of thought, expression, belief, faith and
worship;
  EQUALITY of status and of opportunity;
and to promote among them all
  FRATERNITY assuring the dignity of the individual
and the unity of the Nation;
  IN OUR CONSTITUENT ASSEMBLY this twenty-
sixth day of November, 1949, do HEREBY ADOPT,
ENACT AND GIVE TO OURSELVES THIS
CONSTITUTION.

मूकनायक (Leader of the Voiceless)

EDUCATE, AGITATE, ORGANISE

1891

Born on 14 April in Mhow, Madhya Pradesh. His father is a subedar in the British Indian army.

1900s

They move to Satara. A Brahmin teacher in his school is very fond of him and changes Bhimrao's surname from Ambavadekar to his own, Ambedkar, in the school records.

In 1901, they move to Mumbai, where he is the only one from his caste at Elphinstone High School.

Passes matriculation in 1907, the first boy in his community to do so. His father's friend gifts him his copy of his book on Buddha. Ambedkar is "greatly impressed and moved by it".

1910s

Graduates in 1912. Wins a scholarship from the Gaekwad ruler of Baroda for higher studies at Columbia University, New York.

Arrives in USA in 1913. Takes 29 courses in economics, 11 in history, 6 in sociology, 5 in philosophy, 4 in anthropology, 3 in politics and 1 each in elementary French and German.

Completes two master's degrees in economics. Presents important papers on commerce and caste, and is influenced by John Dewey's work on democracy.

Moves to Britain in 1916 to study law at Gray's Inn. Also enrols for a doctorate at London School of Economics. His scholarship ends at this point and he has to return to India.

A World War I German submarine torpedoes the ship carrying his precious collection of books and papers to India. Loses his dissertation too, and has to rewrite it!

In 1917, is appointed military secretary to the maharaja of Baroda.

In 1918, starts teaching at Sydenham College, Mumbai. Is very popular with the students but some professors still refuse to share their jug of water with him.

In a 1919 survey for the upcoming Montagu-Chelmsford reforms, testifies that "The real social divisions in India are: (1) Touchable Hindus. (2) Untouchable Hindus. (3) Mohammedans. (4) Christians. (5) Parsees. (6) Jews." Argues for separate electorates and reservations for the Untouchable Hindus group.

1920s

Starts the Marathi weekly *Mooknayak* in 1920, the first of his five periodicals, with help from the progressive maharaja of Kolhapur. In the very first issue, calls India "a home of inequality".

Returns to London to finish his legal studies and PhD.

Is back in Mumbai in 1924 as a barrister and part-time lecturer. Establishes the Bahishkrit Hitakarini Sabha for Dalits, with the motto 'Educate, Agitate, Organise'.

In 1925, for the Simon Commission, writes a set of recommendations for the future Constitution of India.

In 1927, leads protest to Chavdar Tank in Mahad, demanding access to water in public spaces. Burns a copy of *Manusmriti*, the book of caste codes for Hindus. Results in further oppression of his followers. Decides it is better to fight through the law than on the streets.

1930s

Invited in 1930–32 to all the Round Table Conferences as a representative of the Dalits.

Is in serious conflict with Gandhi over separate electorate for Dalits. Gandhi fears it will divide Hindus and goes on fast in Yerwada Jail. Finally, the Poona Pact is signed in 1932, where they agree to reserved seats within the electorate for the Depressed Classes, later known as Scheduled Castes and Tribes.

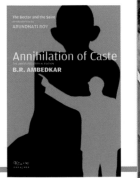

Announces his decision in 1935 to convert to another religion, and asks his followers to do the same.

In 1936, publishes *Annihilation of Caste*, an undelivered speech on the evils of caste — so hard-hitting that alarmed organisers cancelled the conference at which he was to have spoken! The book is a bestseller.

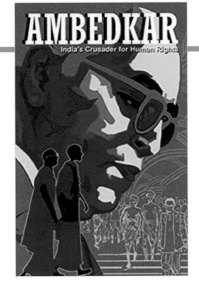

1940s

Becomes a member of the Viceroy's Council in 1942.

After Independence in 1947, is made the law mininster and also chairman of the Constitution Drafting Committee.

1950s

Steered by Ambedkar, the Indian Constitution comes into force on 26 January 1950. India is now a republic with its own laws, of which Article 17 abolishes untouchability.

Resigns from the cabinet in 1951, upset that his Hindu Code Bill giving more rights to women is stalled.

In 1956, in Nagpur, along with thousands of Mahars and Dalits, converts to a new sect of Buddhism that he founds called Navayana, meaning 'new vehicle', for liberation from untouchability. Passes away in Mumbai two months later.

প্রশান্ত চন্দ্র মহলানবিশ

P. C. MAHALANOBIS

1893–1972

To his students, 'PCM' was
Professor of Counting and Measurement! To India,
he was the pioneer of the little known field of statistics,
experimenting with its many uses. Just in time. Because
when the newly independent nation called for a whole new domain
of economic planning, his statistical tools readily became its
foundation. Famous for employing 'human computers' to handle
the large calculations, he was the first to have mechanical
calculating machines and the earliest indigenous computers
designed for India. The statistical institute he set up
became the envy of the world.

PRASANTA CHANDRA MAHALANOBIS waited for news of a ship. The young physics graduate from Cambridge University needed to get back from England to India for a short holiday. Unfortunately for him, it was the summer of 1915, World War I was raging, and ships were delayed due to troop deployment. Never one to waste time, he retreated to the library at King's College. While browsing the shelves, he discovered what was to be life-changing for him as well as for the future of economic planning in independent India.

Mahalanobis had found *Biometrika*, a journal devoted to the theory of statistics, a relatively new subject at the time. Fascinated by what he read, he bought a whole set of nine volumes to read on the voyage home.

After returning to India, Mahalanobis began teaching physics at Presidency College in Kolkata. But by now he was completely absorbed by statistics. He realised that numbers and measurements could be put to practical use for making humans more efficient. He set about actively searching for problems to work on using statistical methods.

Mahalanobis had grown up in Kolkata in a home with a liberal atmosphere, where leading intellectuals and social reformers were regular visitors. He studied literature, philosophy and Sanskrit. He was a personal friend of Rabindranath Tagore, even helping him run his university at Shantiniketan for many years. All this had a great impact on the kind of person he turned out to be. Apart from mathematics and physics, he had a wide range of other interests which he now applied to statistics. He wrote over 200 scientific papers based on numerical data, on topics as far-flung as anthropology, weather patterns and agriculture, to snail shell designs and tea drinking habits among the Indian middle class!

His big break came in the 1920s after devastating floods in Bengal and Odisha. Engineers said that since rainfall had increased over the years, building basins would hold excess rainwater in future. But Mahalanobis analysed data on rainfall and flood patterns of over 50 years and showed that the floods were being caused not by heavier rain, but by blocked drainage systems. Statistics had proved expert engineers wrong! His calculations were later used for planning dam and irrigation projects.

"I discussed with a friend of mine ... the possibility of having a separate section for statistics ... [He] told me that some of his colleagues had remarked: 'If statistics is to have a section, you may as well have a section for astrology' ... The forecasting of future events is, of course, a common feature, and the basis was felt to be equally unscientific ... A great change has taken place in the climate of scientific and public opinion about statistics."

P. C. Mahalanobis at the Indian Science Congress, 1950

"No one in history could achieve anything great unless he was tough, could act boldly with faith in his convictions, and had the ability to argue ... and get things done. Mahalanobis had all these traits in good measure ... Statistical science was a virgin field and practically unknown in India before the twenties ... It needed a pioneer and adventurer like him, with ... courage and tenacity to fight all opposition."

T. J. Rao, statistician

In Presidency College, he began to invite a small, informal group of interested scholars for regular meetings in his room where they discussed the systems and use of statistics. This was the beginning of the famous Indian Statistical Institute (ISI) which came into being a few years later. He had a knack for picking good academic talent, and many of his students and associates went on to great fame.

When Independence came, economists and planners were in despair. India was a poor nation with 350 million people, no proper industries and disorganised agriculture. To frame good socio-economic programmes they needed accurate data. But how were they to collect it from such a vast population without being swamped with information? And how were they to use these numbers?

Mahalanobis was ready. Back in the 1930s, his team had started pilot surveys and sampling methods. Based on this, he introduced the National Sample Survey, one of the most brilliant such large-scale programmes in the world. It gathered data on poverty, household consumption, healthcare and education in carefully designed random samples to accurately represent the large population. Economists were able to quickly use this to frame important schemes to reduce poverty and distribute funds, and for industrialisation and agriculture.

As is usual, not everyone was convinced. Agriculturists could not see how numbers would improve crop yields. Administrators often did not like the idea of being forced to systematically collect information that they could not immediately link to policy decisions. But the prime minister, Jawaharlal Nehru, realised the importance of his work and brought Mahalanobis into economic planning. The statistician used his surveys and practical ideas to guide the Second Five-Year Plan for India, directing the focus onto heavy industry and self-reliance.

Meanwhile, ISI began to receive worldwide recognition, attracting scientists and scholars like Niels Bohr and Andrei N. Kolmogorov to visit and teach. Leaders like Nikita Khrushchev of the USSR came by. Chinese premier Zhou en-Lai was said to be so frustrated with the vast quantities of unusable data his own economists collected that he visited ISI himself, then sent his statisticians to train here.

Mahalanobis wielded statistics like a practical and powerful tool. It was his "arithmetic of human welfare". To him, these were no dry facts and figures — the numbers he dealt with had a human face.

"We are now obsessed with Big Data, and aspire to use it in every aspect of our life – from business to sports. However, when it comes to the delicate question of national policy making, it becomes really serious, as a wrong decision based on potentially inaccurate or insufficient data analytics might have a tremendous impact on the nation.

One needs to be a top-level statistician with immense experience of handling data at the same time to be able to take the right policy decision. Mahalanobis' adventure of paving the way of statistical heritage in India was supplemented by the fact that he himself was a world-class statistician."

Atanu Biswas, ISI professor, 2018

THE FACE OF FIGURES

1893

Born in Kolkata on 29 June, now celebrated as National Statistics Day.

1910s

In 1912, gets a BSc degree from Presidency College, Kolkata, being taught by eminent scientists Jagadish Chandra Bose and Prafulla Chandra Ray.

Goes to England in 1913 for higher studies at the University of London. Visiting a friend at Cambridge, he is so impressed with the place that he ends up studying physics and mathematics in King's College instead. While there, interacts with maths genius Srinivasa Ramanujan.

In 1915, at Cambridge, comes across *Biometrika*, a journal that sparks off a fascination with statistics and its many uses.

1920s

Returns to India in 1922, intending to go back to Cambridge for a doctorate. Begins teaching physics at Presidency College and stays there for the next 33 years.

Sets up a laboratory to research the application of statistics in fields such as economics, anthropology and agriculture. Does a path-breaking project analysing anthropometric data on the Anglo-Indians of Kolkata, a racially mixed group. This is the first time statistics is used to study something like this.

Does a massive study of the cause of floods in Bengal and Odisha, which gives useful inputs for the construction of the Hirakud Dam and Damodar Valley Project later.

1930s

In 1930–31, formulates the D^2 Statistics, known as the Mahalanobis Distance — today widely used for measuring differences between 2 different data sets.

Starts the Indian Statistical Institute (ISI) in 1930 out of the Statistical Laboratory in Presidency College, along with professors P. N. Banerji, N. R. Sen and R. N. Mukherji. It grows over the years to become a premier institution.

In 1933, the ISI starts *Sankhya, The Indian Journal of Statistics*, along the lines of *Biometrika*, with Mahalanobis as editor. Sankhya, he explains, means not just 'number' but 'determinate knowlege', the basis of statistics.

Starts the first of his large-scale sample surveys in 1937, with the acreage and yield of jute crops in Bengal. The technique is considered the most accurate in the world at that time, and is one of his most important contributions to the field of statistics.

In 1938, organises the first statistical conference in India presided over by famous statistician R. A. Fisher.

1940s

ISI does some major large-scale survey and data analyses in varied fields like census, family budgets, traffic flow, coin circulation, crop yield estimation, and even assessing the impact of the famine in Bengal.

In 1943, he sets up the Indian Calculating Machine and Scientific Instrument Research Society for local assembly and manufacture of tabulating devices. ISI has by now a proper workshop for repair and maintenance of calculators.

In 1949, he is appointed honorary statistical advisor to the Indian government. Is asked to play an important role in national economic planning, and in drafting the Second Five-Year Plan.

Made a member of the newly formed United Nations Sub-Commission on Sampling, later the chairman.

1950s

Helps establish the National Sample Survey Organisation (NSSO) and the Central Statistical Office to undertake statistical activities all over India.

Gives a famous speech, 'Why Statistics?', at the Indian Science Congress in 1950, outlining his vision of its role in developing newly independent India.

One of the first to recognise the importance of the brand new field of computers for accurately processing complicated figures. In 1950, starts the Electronic Computer Laboratory at ISI for computer related work.

In 1953, with his encouragement, S. K. Mitra and S. M. Bose design India's first analogue electronic computer — parts of which have been salvaged from the city's junkyards! Nehru pays a visit to see this "wonder".

In 1956, sources and instals at ISI a British-made digital computer, one of just a few available in the world. The HEC-2M is the first of its kind in Asia.

Sets up the Geological Studies Unit at ISI. In 1958, they discover dinosaur bones in the Godavari Valley. The giant skeleton is reassembled, named *Barapasaurus tagorei*, and diplayed at ISI.

By 1959, ISI is a computer centre for the country, computing for the Ministry of Defence, the Atomic Energy Commission and the Meteorology Department.

1960s

Awarded the Padma Vibhushan and the Srinivasa Ramanujan Gold Medal in 1968.

From the 1940s to the 1960s, more than 600 leading scientists, economists and world leaders visit ISI. With a headstart, when statistics as a subject was still very new, it is a model for such institutes the world over. The University of California, Berkeley, starts its statistical laboratory in 1938 and statistics department in 1955, Beijing University in 1956.

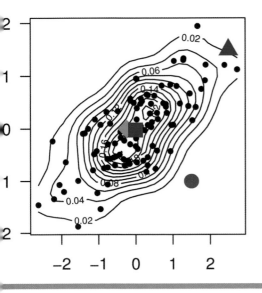

সত্যেন্দ্রনাথ বসু

SATYENDRA NATH BOSE

1894–1974

One of a group of science luminaries
to come out of Calcutta University in the early
20th century, Satyendra Nath Bose gave the world quantum
statistics – a critical foundation of the quantum theory in
physics, and a key contribution to the second scientific revolution.
Albert Einstein himself was the first to recognise its importance!
Despite high international accolades, Bose continued with
his varied scientific explorations, devoting himself to
popularising science in the local language. One half of the
particles that exist in the universe now bear
the name of this modest man.

ALBERT EINSTEIN was a busy man. The world-famous physicist had plenty of demands on his time — research, lab work, lectures, a stream of visitors from around the world, and a mailbox stuffed full with letters, invitations, journals and academic papers that he would probably never get around to reading. But something about the slim package from India caught his attention. It was an article with a note attached.

"Respected Sir," the note began, "I have ventured to send you the accompanying article for your perusal and opinion. I am anxious to know what you think of it. You will see that I have tried to deduce the coefficient $8\,\pi\,v^2/c^3$ in Planck's Law independent of the classical electrodynamics..."

The letter was dated 4 June 1924. The attached four-page article was entitled 'Planck's Law and the Hypothesis of Light Quanta' written by Satyendra Nath Bose, a physics lecturer from Dhaka University. And it was to change the course of quantum physics.

Bose was a maths prodigy. As a child, his father would draw problems for him to solve in the courtyard of their Kolkata home before he left for work. One maths teacher was so dazzled that he gave him 110 out of 100 in a test, for not just solving the given problems but doing so through different methods with several alternatives! There was no class or examination that he did not top right until his master's degree. He and his equally brilliant friend, Meghnad Saha (the famous astrophysicist), grabbed all the academic prizes available at the time.

They both wanted to teach mathematics and physics at the University of Calcutta. But since there was no PhD programme, the vice-chancellor funded a period of research for them in order to upgrade their knowledge of physics.

By 1914, the world of physics was a very exciting place, new concepts challenging classical ideas. But the outbreak of World War I meant that the two friends could not get academic journals they required from Europe. Funds were limited, with no library to speak of. They determinedly went through a period of intense self-study, even learning German and French to read cutting-edge academic books borrowed from an Austrian scientist in Kolkata. And they surprised everyone by translating Albert Einstein's work on general relativity into English!

"Eric Weiner in his best-selling book *The Geography of Genius: A Search for the World's Most Creative Places from Ancient Athens to Silicon Valley*, writes how 'Certain places, at certain times, produced a bumper crop of brilliant minds and good ideas', and includes Calcutta (1840–1920) in the list of these places ... In the field of science, this period saw the emergence of C. V. Raman, S. N. Bose and Meghnad Saha, the likes of which has not happened in the country since then. Many factors must have contributed to such a flourishing environment – [one being] the urge for self-expression in a country reeling under colonial rule."
Amitabha Bhattacharya, ex-IAS officer and writer, 2019

Bose moved to Dhaka University, making a name for himself as a dedicated teacher. He made sure to understand every concept he taught his students. It was while preparing for a lecture on Max Planck's law of radiation that he found himself a little confused.

Max Planck, a German physicist, had introduced the revolutionary idea of quantum physics saying that energy was made of tiny individual units or quanta. However, Bose found himself disagreeing with the way the law had been proved in mathematical terms. He developed his own way of counting these microparticles or photons to prove Planck's law in a much more suitable way. He wrote a paper on his discovery and sent it to the London science journal, *Philosophical Magazine*. It was rejected.

So, in an inspired move, he wrote directly to Albert Einstein with not much hope of ever hearing from the great man.

Einstein was not just impressed by what he read, he translated it himself and had it published in a prestigious German journal! Bose's short paper started a whole new field known as quantum statistics, and this new way of counting some of the fundamental particles that make up matter came to be known as Bose-Einstein statistics. Einstein later remarked that Bose's work was "the fourth and last of the revolutionary papers of the old quantum theory", placing him on a par with legendary physicists Max Planck, Neils Bohr and Albert Einstein himself!

Bose now found himself quite a celebrity in the world of science. He travelled to Europe, meeting and working with the greatest scientific minds of the century, including Marie Curie and his hero, Einstein.

An entirely self-taught physicist, Bose never got his PhD. Nor did he get the Nobel Prize that many said he deserved, although Bose-Einstein statistics was used as the base of many Nobel Prize winning works in later years. He continued as the committed teacher, passionate about education, known for his love of poetry, chess and playing his favourite esraj — and his special fondness for cats!

But when he died, the entire route of his hearse was lined with crowds who had come to honour him — a send-off worthy of a Nobel winner.

"S. Chandrasekhar [astrophysicist] recounts an incident in 1928 when he visited [C. V.] Raman, his uncle, in Calcutta. Bose, after seeing Raman's results, prophesied, 'Professor Raman, you have made a great discovery. It will be called Raman effect, and you will get the Nobel Prize' ... Chandrasekhar also remarked, 'Bose, in some ways, from the human point of view, was the best of them all. He was very generous, gentle, easy-going, and not particularly caring about the glamorous aspects of science.'"

Amitabha Bhattacharya, ex-IAS officer and writer, 2019

"He used to work out detailed and distinctly written out steps of calculations on sheets of paper with meticulous care when he gave us courses on X-ray crystallography *in our mother tongue Bengali* ... in a branch of physics which was not even his main field of interest."

Purnima Sinha, Bose's doctoral student in the early 1950s

Planck's Law and the Hypothesis of Light Quanta

by Satyendra Nath Bose

Respected Sir,

I have ventured to send you the accompanying article for your perusal and opinion. I am anxious to know what you think of it. You will see that I have tried to deduce the coefficient $\frac{8\pi v^2}{c^3}$ in Planck's Law independent of classical electrodynamics.

from a letter to Albert Einstein

বিজ্ঞান

THE MAN WHO COUNTED PHOTONS

1894

Born on 1 January in Kolkata. His father, an accountant with a love for science and maths, recognises and encourages his son's exceptional maths ability.

1909

Joins Presidency College for an intermediate in science. Jagadish Chandra Bose and Prafulla Chandra Ray are some very inspiring teachers. His classmate Jnan Chandra Ghosh goes on to become a well known scientist.

1910s

Tops the intermediate exam in 1911, winning the Duff Scholarship for proficiency in physics.

Enrols for bachelors in the same college. Meets Meghnad Saha, who later becomes a famous astrophysicist. They become research partners and lifelong friends.

Tops BSc and MSc in applied mathematics with record breaking marks, prizes and gold medals.

Calcutta University has no PhD programmes as yet. With funding from the vice-chancellor, in 1916 he and Saha start a period of independent research to set up a postgraduate programme in maths and physics.

Quantum physics and Max Planck have recently marked their presence in Europe. Bose and Saha source books from Paul Brühl, an Austrian teaching at Bengal Engineering College, and learn scientific French and German to understand them.

At the end of 1916, Bose becomes a lecturer at the University.

In 1918, *Philosophical Magazine* publishes his first important joint paper with Saha in theoretical physics.

In 1919, he and Saha publish *The Principle of Relativity: original papers by A. Einstein and H. Minowski...* with an introduction by P. C. Mahalanobis. This is the first English translation of Einstein's work.

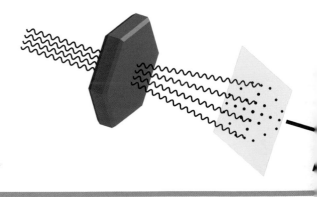

1920s

Appointed Reader in the physics department at the newly opened University of Dhaka (now in Bangladesh) in 1921. Sets up a whole new department and laboratories.

In 1924, writes to Albert Einstein with his own derivation of Planck's quantum radiation law. Einstein translates the paper himself into German and has it published in *Zeitschrift für Physik*. Tells Bose it is "an important step forward and I liked it very much".

The paper creates the new area of quantum statistics, and is now considered most important in quantum theory.

Travels to France and Germany in 1924-26 to work alongside scientists, including Marie Curie and Einstein.

Einstein uses Bose statistics to predict the Bose-Einstein Condensate.

Returns to Dhaka University in 1926. Armed with a letter of recommendation from Einstein himself, is appointed professor and head of the physics department.

1937

Rabindranath Tagore dedicates *Visva Parichay* ('Introduction to the Universe'), his only book on science, to Bose.

1945

With Partition imminent, he returns to the University of Calcutta. Is there until 1956, working and researching in biology, mineralogy, organic chemistry and nuclear physics among other areas. Insists that his students design their own equipment using local materials and technicians.

The Principle of Relativity; Original Papers by A. Einstein and H. Minkowski. Translated into English by M.N. Saha and S.N. Bose; With a Historical Introd. by P.C. Mahalanobis

Scholar
SELECT

ALBERT EINSTEIN, HERMANN MINKOWSKI

1946

Scientist Paul Dirac coins the word 'boson' to describe one of the two groups of particles that make up the subatomic universe, the other being fermions. This is in honour of Bose's contribution to quantum statistics.

1948

Believing it is important to teach science in the mother tongue, Bose launches the Bangiya Vijnan Parishad to popularise and promote science in Bengali. Gives free classes to underprivileged children to promote education and the scientific temper for national development.

1954

Awarded the Padma Vibhushan.

Nominated to the Rajya Sabha.

1956

Nominated for the Nobel Prize in Physics for his contribution to the Bose-Einstein statistics, but does not win. "I have got all the recognition I deserve," he says.

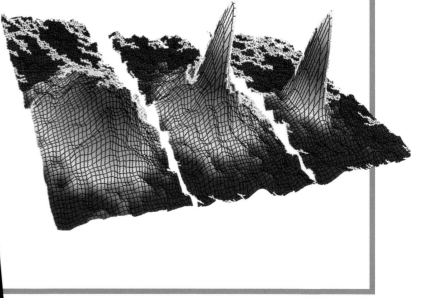

కొట్టారి కనకయ్య నాయుడు

C. K. NAYUDU

1895–1967

A bold stance. Long, lofted sixes cracking
off his straight bat. C. K. Nayudu did not believe
in only winning, he believed in demolishing the opposition.
At a time when cricket was a game of leisure, or played against its
English inventors confident of their superior skills, his aggressive
style forced a new respect for Indian cricket. It announced that
India was ready to meet the world on equal terms. An emerging
nation agreed – huge numbers cheered every shot,
treating each of his triumphs as a harbinger
of their own bright future.

THE VISITORS WERE ALL-OUT for 363. On day two, a slightly shaky home team was at 67 for 2 when CK strode out to the crease. He stood there, all strapping six-foot-two of him, glowering at the bowler — and on the third ball, swung an aggressive bat, lofting it onto the roof of the Bombay Gymkhana. The crowd went wild! This was no ordinary sixer. It was the beginning of the most important innings in the history of Indian cricket.

Cricket came to India with the British. At first, it was considered a game for the elite, played for leisure by British administrators and officials. The only Indians who had access to the game were either nawabs or maharajas. By the early 20th century, interest in the game had risen. Indians of all backgrounds took to the game and there was a growing number of spectators. In 1911, there was even an 'All-India' side which toured England. But the British did not really consider the Indians serious competition. How could recent learners match the inventors of the game? India was, after all, still a colony.

Cottari Kanakaiya Nayudu — CK, as he was known — had other ideas. His family worked for the Holkar rulers in Nagpur. It was here that CK learnt his cricket. He started playing First Class matches in the community-based Quadrangular tournament in Mumbai. This was an early version of the Ranji Trophy where teams were named after communities — Hindus, Muslims, Parsees, Europeans. With his superb fitness and great discipline, he developed into a fearless batsman with added all-round skills as an off-spinner and a brilliant fielder. It helped that he towered over everyone and sported a rather fierce appearance that managed to intimidate his opponents even before he started playing!

Around this time, the first waves of the Independence movement were being felt around the country. Patriotic feelings were running high, but along with it, a need for Indians to believe in themselves, to feel that they could indeed challenge their oppressors in any field and win.

Which is why, when the crowds swarmed the Bombay Gymkhana grounds on 1 December 1926, there was more at stake than just a cricket match.

They were there to watch the Marylebone Cricket Club team from England take on the Hindus. The MCC team was fresh from a string of victories in Karachi,

"...every six hit by Nayudu against the visitors was as good as a nail in the coffin of the British Empire ... We madly cheered each shot past the boundary not only as a cricket performance but also as an assertion of our resolve to throw the British out of India."
A student in the crowds at the Lahore match against MCC in 1933

"There was Palwankar Baloo, whose career mirrored the tortuous struggle against that most pernicious of human institutions, Untouchability. There was C. K. Nayudu, who depsite himself came to embody the hopes of a nation-in-the-making. Now there was Azhar [Mohammed Azharuddin], who came to carry in his person and in his career the fears of a nation in uncertain middle age [because of his religion]."
Ramachandra Guha, in *A Corner of a Foreign Field: The Indian History of a British Sport*, on the symbolic and social significance of cricket

Rawalpindi, Lahore and Ajmer. Similar results were expected here. Only, the visitors had not factored in the formidable talent of CK.

The cracking sixer was just the beginning. By lunch, news had spread of the ongoing display. People from all corners of the city abandoned their work and crowded the venue, craning their necks from rooftops and treetops to catch a glimpse of CK's spectacular innings. It was almost as if they sensed that this was history in the making. Spurred on by the cheering crowds, CK scored a scorching 153 in 116 minutes with 11 sixes and 13 fours! When he finally walked to the pavilion, fans threw garlands of flowers and gifts at him, jostling to try and catch a glimpse or even touch the man of the moment. The message was clear — a non-royal, who had learned and played all his cricket in India, had proved that the English were not invincible.

Thanks to CK's innings that day, India made Test status and he went on to captain India in its first Test at Lord's in 1932. Wherever he played, crowds would turn out to cheer. Every hard-hitting shot was seen as a blow against the British Empire.

Listed in *Wisden Cricketer's Almanack,* and compared with Don Bradman, CK was now a national hero of sorts. Legends built up of how far his shots could go. One story had it that in England he had hit a ball into the next county. In another match, a commentator remarked that the ball was "last seen sailing in an easterly direction". Fans waited to shower him with flowers and currency notes. Selectors were publicly questioned when they dared drop him from the team.

Appointed a colonel in the Holkar army, CK cut a dashing figure in his dress uniform, driving around in his Rolls-Royce. Beneath the cool exterior, he was very disciplined and a hard taskmaster. He demanded high standards as the coach of the highly successful Holkar state team — players were not even allowed a drink of water on the field. This was no surprise considering CK himself was known to have played through injury and illness!

CK's cricket records may not sound as impressive as those of Sunil Gavaskar or Sachin Tendulkar or Virat Kohli. But many consider him the first great Indian cricketer. With his bold approach to the game, he gave an aspiring nation a spring in its step.

"Nayudu's innings marked a paradigm shift in the way Indian cricket was perceived. The English had come expecting to win most matches easily, and to find the occasional pocket of resistance which they would patronisingly applaud later, after having brushed it aside. But on that day in December, Nayudu did not resist – he destroyed. He did not stand firm – he annihilated. He showed no respect to the opposition and in doing so, earned respect for Indian cricket."

Amit Varma, journalist, 2002

"...the entire Indian team visited my house ... It shows the impact my dad has made on the game and their careers. Visiting Ranji teams also come to meet me. They want to have a look at my dad's bat and cricketing gear."

Chandra Nayudu, CK's daughter and one of the first women commentators in India, 2016

1932 Indian Test Cricket Team

BUY!

BATHGATE LIVER TONIC

BATHGATE
LIVER TONIC
yum yum yum

CRICKET'S FIRST COLOSSUS

1895

Born on 31 October in Nagpur, Maharashtra, into a land owning family from Andhra Pradesh working for the ruling Holkars of Indore.

Makes his cricket debut at age 7 in the school team of Hislop Collegiate High School.

1916

Starts First Class cricket in the Bombay Quadrangular tournament. Performs well for his Hindus team.

1920s

In 1923, Tukoji Rao III, the ruler of Indore, invites him to play for the Holkar team. He is made a captain in the Holkar State Army. Later is promoted to colonel.

Plays an iconic match for the Hindus at the Bombay Gymkhana against Arthur Gilligan's MCC team in 1926 — hits 153 runs in 116 minutes with 11 sixes. MCC presents him with a silver bat in recognition.

With this match India is established in cricket, and made a Full Member of the Imperial Cricket Conference (ICC).

The Indian Cricket Board is formed in 1928, a consortium of state cricket associations.

1930s

India plays its first ever Test in 1932, a one-off match against England at Lord's. The maharaja of Porbandar, Natwarsinhji Bhavsinhji is selected as captain but falls ill, leaving CK to lead the team as India's first Test captain.

A crowd of 24,000, including the king, gather to watch the Lord's Test. The English team, helmed by the legendary Douglas Jardine, wins. But CK hits the highest score of 40 in the first innings despite a hand injury while fielding.

In a match at Edgbaston in the same tour, he clobbers a ball more than 73 m over the square boundary. It lands in the River Rea, technically crossing from the county of Warwickshire into Worcestershire!

In 1933, is named one of *Wisden*'s Cricketers of the Year.

In 1933-34, India hosts its first ever Test series, a 3-match tour against England. The first match is at the Bombay Gymkhana grounds, where over 50,000 people turn out to watch. England wins the series 2-0. But CK's bowling figures of 4/21 in the second match at Eden Gardens, Kolkata, results in one match at least being a draw.

1940s

From the early 1940s, leads the Holkar team to 8 Ranji Trophy finals in 9 seasons, with 4 wins.

In 1941, becomes the first Indian cricketer to endorse a brand — Bathgate Liver Tonic.

1950s

Controversy erupts in 1952 when, as chairman of the Selection Committee, CK refuses to assure the great all-rounder Vinoo Mankad of a place in the Indian team to counter an offer from Lancashire League, UK.

Awarded the Padma Bhushan in 1955.

Plays his last Ranji Tropy in 1956-57, scoring 52 for Uttar Pradesh at age 62.

1960s

His final match is for charity, in 1963-64, playing for the Maharashtra Governor's XI against the Maharashtra Chief Minister's XI. He is now almost 70 years old!

His career spans a phenomenal 50 years, with 7 Tests in which he scores 350 runs and takes 9 wickets. In his 207 First Class matches, he scores over 10,000 runs and takes 411 wickets.

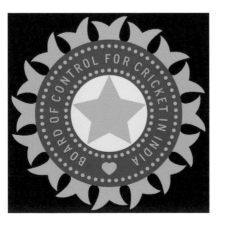

ಕಮಲಾದೇವಿ ಭಟ್ಟೋಪಾಧ್ಯಾಯ್

KAMALADEVI CHATTOPADHYAY

1903–1988

More than once, she was called
"a dangerous woman"! Perhaps because Kamaladevi
never hesitated to rock the boat when it came to defying convention.
She persuaded Gandhi to back a more active role for women during Civil
Disobedience, leading to a revolution within the movement – Indian
women coming out of their homes, picketing shops, shouting slogans,
facing lathi blows and jail sentences. She insisted that women be
recognised as equal participants in everything. A dynamic trailblazer
pre-Independence, she refused political office later,
dedicating herself instead to craftspeople and their
crafts, and shaping India's cultural life.

CAN YOU GO TO JAIL for selling a packet of salt?

In pre-Independence India it was possible.

Kamaladevi knew it would happen. And yet, it was she who persuaded Gandhi to allow women to participate in the Salt Satyagraha. The year was 1930. Mahatma Gandhi had just launched the Civil Disobedience movement against British rule. The first step was to defy a ridiculous law that did not allow Indians to make or sell salt, a basic commodity. Instead, even the poorest person had to buy expensive, often imported, salt.

Although Gandhi wanted to highlight a problem that affected the maximum number of citizens, he was initially reluctant to have women participate. It was only on Kamaladevi's insistence that he finally relented and called on the women of India to take part in the non-violent struggle.

So while he led the famous Dandi March in Gujarat, in faraway Mumbai huge crowds gathered on Chowpatty Beach. At the forefront was the young, plucky Kamaladevi Chattopadhyay. In full view of the enraged authorities, thousands of men, women and children set up makeshift stoves and pans on the beach, carrying sea water to boil down to make salt!

But soon enough, the police arrived with their lathis and big boots and began to mercilessly lash out at the crowds, trying to disperse them. Kamaladevi was hit. She fell against the hot coals of a stove, badly burning her arm. She refused to be moved, however, worried instead for a young man right next to her who had his skull cracked by a police lathi. Blows and kicks rained down from all directions, but she stood firm, gathering as much of the salt from the pans as she could.

Looking back on the event, she wrote, "It seemed such a stupendous moment in my life and in the life of the women of my country." She was thrilled that, for the first time, ordinary women had come out of their homes to take part in a political campaign.

There was more to come.

Kamaladevi appeared at the Bombay Share Bazaar where, to cries of "Mahatma Gandhi ki jai", she auctioned the collected salt to enthusiastic brokers and clerks.

"The application of this concept of satyagraha as a political weapon was startling and exciting. It was like viewing a new instrument, simple yet promising to be powerful in operation."
Kamaladevi Chattopadhyay

"She was the first woman in the country to stand for elections. In her address, at the Clock Tower Maidan, Bangalore, at the age of 23, she had the conviction to say, 'If you vote for me, it won't be a personal favour, you will be paying homage to womankind at large' ... When everyone who called themselves as revolutionaries only spoke, she was in jail demanding minimum facilities for female inmates."
Devaki Jain, economist, writer, and Kamaladevi's friend, 2018

Some of the packets were marked 'Gandhi Salt. Price: Six months jail'. And then, much to everyone's delight, she cheekily walked into the High Court and asked the dumbstruck magistrates if they were interested in buying the illegal Gandhi Salt! The volunteers made more than 50,000 rupees that day — a huge amount of money at the time.

The authorities soon realised that they were up against a very determined adversary. Bold and defiant, she was a great motivator and organiser, and clearly needed to be put out of the way. On the eve of another great raid on the salt pans of Wadala, outside Mumbai, Kamaladevi was apprehended, becoming the first woman to be arrested in the Independence movement. She was given a long sentence. The judge felt she was responsible for more people breaking the law than almost anyone else. Kamaladevi scoffed at the idea — she found it amusing that the mighty British Empire should so fear a 27-year-old woman, a single mother with a seven-year-old son.

From her privileged upbringing in a genteel, highly educated family from Mangaluru to jail was certainly a long journey. But it was just the beginning of almost 50 years of untiring service to her country, often at great personal cost.

She travelled all over the world, mingling with great leaders and common folk alike, cutting an elegant figure in her handloom saris and beautiful jewellery made by the artisans of India. She talked and wrote with great passion on India's struggle for freedom, creating a just world order, women's and workers' rights, and methods of non-violent civil disobedience.

After Independence, she turned down all offers of public office. Instead, she worked to resettle the refugees who had spilled over the borders after Partition. Later, using her superb organisational skills and her love of the arts, she set up a national handicrafts board, a crafts museum, and theatre and music and dance academies, all of which are the hub of India's cultural life today.

It is difficult to imagine one person doing all this in a lifetime. She was sometimes light-heartedly called "the uncrowned queen of India". She preferred to describe herself as a "sepoy and a sevika" — a soldier and a server.

"…it was these dynamic women [Kamaladevi and Sarojini Naidu] who fought for women's participation in the political arena as equal partners. Their active participation in the freedom struggle was closely linked with women's rights and thus they were able to get support, often grudgingly given, to the women's cause."

Jasleen Dhamija, textile art historian and Kamaladevi's colleague, 2016

"What she had written in 1939 on Imperialism and class struggle was suggestive of … how national struggle had led to a closer union between the British and Indian capitalists. She whispered into my ears on the first Republic Day as Rajendra Prasad was taken on a royal chariot, 'Don't you see, Devaki, how we are imitating the British? President of independent India goes on a procession just like the British and stays at the same building where the Governor General lived.'"

Devaki Jain, economist, writer, and Kamaladevi's friend, 2018

"I came to understand the deep relationship of handicrafts with our daily life...to live with them and make them an integral part of our everyday existence"

GANDHI SALT

price: 6 months jail

CRAFTING INDIA

1903

Born on 3 April in Mangaluru, to a family that is intellectual and political. Grows up influenced by two educated, strong women — her mother and grandmother. Family troubles make her realise as a child that "women have no rights".

1917

Gets married and is widowed two years later, when she moves to Chennai to study further.

1920s

At 20, defying orthodox taboos against widows remarrying, she marries poet-dramatist Harindranath Chattopadhyay — Sarojini Naidu's brother — under the liberal 1872 Marriage Act that allows widow remarriage as well as inter-caste and inter-community marriage.

Performs in folk and regional theatre along with her husband, again against social norms. Theatre is "like a crusade that drew from people's everyday lives," she says.

Goes to Bedford College in London to study sociology.

Is drawn to the freedom movement by Gandhi's support of indigo farmers. In 1923, enlists with Seva Dal. Recruits and trains hundreds of sevikas, women volunteers of the freedom movement — soon called the Orange Brigade because she changes their sari-uniform from "dull" blue-black to a cheerful orange!

Inspired by theosophist-feminist Margaret Cousins, becomes the first Indian woman to contest for political office when she runs for the Madras Provincial Legislative Council in 1926. Campaigns on women's rights. Loses by just 55 votes.

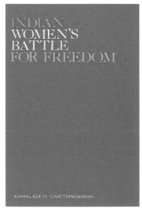

In 1927, formally joins the Congress party.

Cousins founds the All India Women's Conference (AIWC). Kamaladevi is a secretary, later president. Advocates for Child Marriage Restraint, Age of Consent Bill, the Uniform Civil Code to protect women's rights, and to start a Family Planning Association.

Attends the International Alliance of Women in Berlin in 1929, with Sarojini Naidu. Seeing that all countries have their own flag except India, they tear up their silk saris and create one overnight with strips of orange, white and green.

1930s

In 1930, takes part in the Salt Satyagraha protest in Mumbai, and is sent to Pune's Yerwada Jail. Her holding bravely onto the Indian flag in a police scuffle is one of the most striking images of the freedom struggle.

Breaks convention again in 1931 by acting in a movie — *Mrichchhakatika*, the first Kannada silent film.

In 1932, the government sees the disciplined and active Seva Dal as a threat and bans it. Arrests Kamaladevi.

AIWC takes on the bold task of improving women's education. It sponsors and establishes Lady Irwin College for Home Science, New Delhi.

Kamaladevi inaugurates the All India Peasants and Workers Conference in 1935, speaking up for their right to land.

In 1936, takes over as head of the Congress Socialist Party.

Sets off abroad in 1939 for about two years, to attend women's rights conferences and win political support for India.

Key figure in the international feminist movement, but realises while some issues are the same world over, India cannot follow the Western template.

1947–1950s

Post-Independence, she founds the Indian Cooperative Union to build houses for Partition refugees through community development, in what is now Faridabad. Encourages craft based livelihoods for them.

Starts restoring Indian handicrafts and handlooms — travels around the country to meet artisans and encourage them not to give up their skills. Revives the Central Cottage Industries Emporium and sets up state emporiums and an All India Handicrafts Board that she heads for 20 years.

1964

Starts the Crafts Council of India, which today has its prestigious outlets named 'Kamala' after her.

1979

Becomes the first vice-president, later chairperson, of the Sangeet Natak Akademi.

1986

Publishes her autobiography, *Inner Recesses and Outer Spaces*, the last of 18 books written by her on politics, women, society, crafts and theatre.

1987

Conferred the Padma Vibhushan.

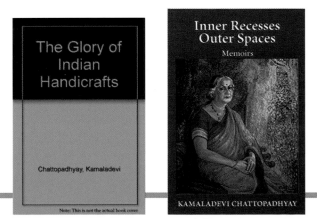

ருக்மிணி தேவி அருண்டேல்

RUKMINI DEVI ARUNDALE

1904–1986

Her name carries with it the
grace of bharatanatyam. Drawn by the beauty of
the temple dance sadir which was sliding into disrepute, she
recreated it with the respectability of tradition. She then redefined
stage and costume aesthetics, and created a storm by publicly
performing herself. Aged just 32, she set up Kalakshetra,
a 'domain of the arts' that helped establish bharatanatyam as a
prominent dance form. This was Rukmini Devi Arundale.
Iconoclastic dancer, institution builder, educationist,
animal rights champion, international icon and,
above all, a daring visionary.

"WOULD YOU LIKE to be President?"

"President of what?"

"President of India."

"Thanks. But no!"

Not many people would have had the conviction to turn down an offer like that. But Rukmini Devi Arundale was all about conviction. So in 1977, when Prime Minister Morarji Desai offered her the post of president of India, the first woman nominated to the Rajya Sabha did not hesitate too much over an answer. There were other things that required her attention.

Rukmini Devi grew up under the unconventional influence of the Theosophical Society, Chennai, with a wide exposure to the great spiritual and artistic heritage of India. Annie Besant, the international president of the Society and a leading light of the freedom movement, became a mentor.

When Rukmini Devi was 16, she shocked Chennai society by marrying an Englishman more than 20 years older than her — educator and fellow theosophist George Sydney Arundale. They both began to travel all over the world as representatives of the Theosophists. In Europe, the young Rukmini immersed herself in the world of arts — theatre, music, painting and opera. Her favourite was dance, to her a "fascinating world of movement and expression".

She was mesmerised by the performances of the legendary ballet dancer, Anna Pavlova. Much to her delight, on a voyage to Australia she found Anna among her co-passengers, along with her entire entourage of dancers and hundreds of pet birds! They spent long hours chatting about dance, and Anna instructed the chief soloist of the troupe to teach her. And so, Rukmini Devi took her first dancing steps in ballet! But something Anna said always stayed with her — to seek inspiration from the beautiful dances of India.

In 1933, Rukmini Devi attended a performance of sadir at the Madras Music Academy. Sadir was an ancient dance form associated with devadasis who traditionally danced in temples. Over the centuries, it had begun to be looked

"I like to go about barefoot. How could I have done that in Rashtrapati Bhavan? I detest arms and armaments. How could I have moved about with an AdC bearing guns in front of me and another behind me? And also as a committed vegetarian how could I have served meat to guests from abroad who cannot do without it…? Besides my life is bound up with Kalakshetra, the Theosophical Society, Madras. Delhi is … another universe…"
Rukmini Devi Arundale

"…she learned ballet not with the idea of becoming a full-fledged dancer. It was just to train [her] body and more for the sheer joy of learning something beautiful."
Avanthi Meduri, ed. *Rukmini Devi Arundale, 1904–1986*

down upon and the dancers were considered women of 'ill repute'. But Rukmini Devi was completely fascinated by what she saw.

She knew what she had to do. She began searching for a teacher to learn sadir. Once again, Chennai society was scandalised. Upper caste girls did not dance, certainly not by learning from devadasis. But she was determined. Finally, the famous guru P. Meenakshisundaram Pillai began, rather reluctantly, to teach her. He insisted she practise every day, 12 hours at a stretch with just an hour's break.

On 30 December 1935, she gave her first public performance at the annual convention of the Theosophical Society. An audience of over a thousand gathered to watch — a few supportive, some curious, others scornful and hostile. They all went back stunned by what they saw. Rukmini Devi had reinvented the form of sadir, by now renamed bharatanatyam, to give it a timeless, spiritual, classical feel.

She did not stop there. She began to change the presentation of the dance itself. The songs and lyrics were now more devotional. Musicians were seated instead of following the dancer around on stage. She studied Indian art and sculpture for references, and then used the help of professional designers to make exquisite costumes and jewellery. Even the stage settings and lighting were tastefully redone, giving the audience a visual treat.

Establishing bharatanatyam as a dominant classical dance form, she now wanted to spread its learning. But first she had to work very hard to change attitudes that frowned upon dance, not taking pride in a great tradition. To her, sustaining the cultural creativity of India was just as important as the fight for Independence.

So she and her husband set up a dance academy — Kalakshetra. Here, classes were held under trees and in simple, thatch-roof studios. She persuaded outstanding musicians and dance gurus to join as teachers. Performances of her beautifully choreographed dance dramas were held on a specially built stage accompanied by respected classical musicians.

Things did not always run smoothly. But there was now a growing respect for Rukmini Devi's dedication to nurture India's artistic traditions.

Occupying the highest office in the land would simply have distracted her from her mission!

"She wasn't training us just to be dancers. Time and again she would tell us to be good citizens, good human beings. Her approach was educational. She was not hell bent upon showing overt sringaram to draw a particular crowd ... dance was another vehicle, like craft or weaving, to have a sense of oneness with oneself ... She set all encompassing syllabi for the arts – textiles, crafts, music, temples, mythology, philosophy…"

Leela Samson, bharatanatyam dancer, Rukmini Devi's student, and ex-director of Kalakshetra, 2010

"...we inherited a set of institutions from our 'national movement', which enshrined the idea of artistic renaissance as integral to the idea of 'freedom'. Rabindranath Tagore [Shantiniketan], Mahakavi Vallathol [Kalamandalam], Rukmini Devi Arundale [Kalakshetra] and Uday Shankar [Uday Shankar Dance and Music Academy] were thus among the first few who built iconic institutions that amplified the idea of freedom to also include the freedom of imagination."

Sadanand Menon, culture critic, 2012

Theosophical
Society

Kalakshetra

A VISION OF DANCE

1904

Born on 29 February in Madurai, to an upper class Tamil Brahmin family. Her mother is a musician, and father an engineer, scholar and theosophist — "very forward thinking" who "disliked many of the narrow prejudices, the caste distinctions ... which were part of our religion in those days".

1912

Her family moves to settle in Adyar, Chennai, near the Theosophical Society. She grows up in an open atmosphere with liberal ideas, meeting people from all over the world.

1918

In her first brief stage appearance, she sings a song in a Tamil version of Tagore's play *Malini*, directed by Eleanor Elder, an Englishwoman at the Society.

1920s

In 1920, scandalises society when she marries George Sydney Arundale, 24 years older, an educationist and theosophist. Her family fully supports her.

Travels abroad with him meeting interesting people, including educator Maria Montessori. Sees ballerina Anna Pavlova perform for the first time in London.

Becomes the president of the All-India Federation of Young Theosophists in 1923, and of the World Federation 2 years later.

In 1927, her brothers take her to a sadir performance by two sisters. Wonderstruck, she feels she is "ushered into a new world of rhythmic beauty and meaning".

Sees Anna Pavlova perform again in Mumbai in 1928. Later, on a ship to Australia, Rukmini Devi is introduced to ballet by Anna Pavlova's lead dancer Cleo Nordi.

1930s

In 1933, she is invited to a sadir performance at Madras Music Academy by E. Krishna Iyer who is fighting to save the ancient dance form. Determined after this to learn the dance, she first persuades Mylapore Gowri Ammal and then Pandanallur Meenakshisundaram Pillai to be her guru.

She and George Arundale start the Besant Theosophical High School in 1934, to honour Annie Besant's wish for a school that gives education without fear. The first Montessori schools in India are set up when they invite Maria Montessori to start courses in this school.

With just a year of learning, gives her first performance at Adyar Theatre for the Diamond Jubilee Convention of the Theosophical Society in 1935. Stuns everyone with her dance, and creates history in Tamil society as the first non-devadasi to dance on stage.

For this and other shows, she has her constumes designed by Madame Cazan, an Italian.

In 1936, with George Arundale, starts Kalakshetra. It is an academy for arts education and training, like a gurukul, passing on skills to the next generation.

Kalakshetra comes a few years after a similar effort in Kerala by Kalamandalam to revive kathakali, kudiyattam and mohiniyattam.

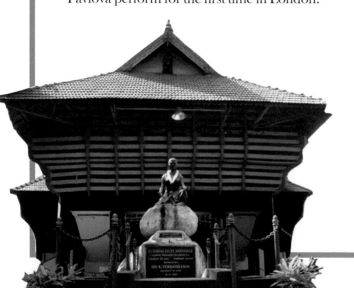

Other outstanding dancers of the time like Balasaraswati and Kumbakonam K. Bhanumathi also perform temple dances on stage. With Rukmini Devi structuring the curriculum at Kalakshetra to bring this dance to the public domain, there is some criticism about it getting standardised.

Starts a weaving centre at Kalakshetra to revive the craft, and give jobs to weavers who are out of work with the arrival of British-made cloth. Brings back traditional designs, colours and motifs into weaves.

1947

The Madras Devadasis Act, introduced in 1928 by the iconic Dr Muthulakshmi Reddi, is passed banning the devadasi system. Sadir as a temple art form is outlawed. Some devadasis object, seeing it as belittling their art and taking away their livelihood.

1950s–70s

First woman to be made a member of the Rajya Sabha in 1952. A passionate animal lover, she introduces and spearheads the passing of the Prevention of Cruelty to Animals Act.

In 1955, becomes vice-president of the International Vegetarian Union, continues for 31 years.

Awarded the Padma Bhushan in 1956.

Given the Sangeet Natak Akademi Award in 1957.

In 1962, is first chairperson of the Animal Welfare Board.

In 1977, refuses the post of President of India so she can continue with her work at Kalakshetra.

1986

'Athai' (aunt) to all at Kalakshtera, she passes away leaving behind over 30 dance dramas that are still performed exactly the way she had wanted them.

1993

An Act passed by parliament recognises Kalakshetra as an Institute of National Importance.

ध्यान चन्द

DHYAN CHAND

1905–1979

Cricket was a game for
rajas and sahibs. It was hockey that emerged
from army cantonments to huge popularity among
ordinary people. Chafing under a colonial yoke, India sent
a team to compete internationally with limited means and expectations.
Dhyan Chand ensured they came home with three consecutive Olympic
hockey golds, and a reputation for being unbeatable. And so it was for
the next three decades! Still considered the ultimate hockey
brain of all time, his mastery of tactics and skills gave
India a national identity in the sporting world,
and put it on the world map.

THE BERLIN OLYMPICS, 1936.

Adolf Hitler sits glowering in the stands. Things are not going well. This was meant to be *his* Olympics. One in which he could showcase the might of the German state, proving to the gathered world the superiority of the so-called Aryan race. But his twisted plans are rapidly coming unstuck thanks to one determined Indian and his team.

The hockey finals between India and Germany start on a sombre note for the Indians. Overnight rains have made the grounds slippery and downright dangerous. The Indians are still smarting from the 4–1 defeat the Germans handed them in a 'friendly' match the day they arrived in Berlin after an exhausting 15-day journey from India. The Germans are all pumped up and soon score their first goal. They play rough and one man is the target. Captain Dhyan Chand loses a tooth. In injury time, he whips off his socks and spiked shoes and returns to the field with only a pair of rubber-soled shoes on his feet! Now, with a better grip on the soggy ground, he completely turns the game around. Running circles round his opponents and rapidly hammering in three goals, he guides his team to a resounding 8–1 victory over the Germans. The Olympic gold is India's.

Hitler is said to have stormed out of the stadium in a fury.

There is a story, that Dhyan Chand was later offered a job in the German army by Hitler himself, which he politely turned down. Another legend has it that he once won a match using a ladies' walking stick. The Dutch are said to have deliberately broken his stick because they were convinced it held a magnet inside which made the ball stick to it. There is talk of a statue of Dhyan Chand somewhere in Austria with four arms and four legs, as a tribute to his phenomenal skills and speed on the hockey field.

Are any of these stories true?

No one knows. And no one seems to challenge them because Dhyan Chand was the kind of person who might well have had any or all of these experiences.

What is certain is that he was a hockey genius.

"You are doubtless aware that I am a common man, and then a soldier. It has been my training from my childhood to avoid limelight and publicity."
Dhyan Chand, in the first line of his autobiography, *Goal*

"His real talent lay above his shoulders. His was easily the hockey brain of the century. He could see a field the way a chess player sees the board. He knew where his teammates were, and more importantly where his opponents were, without looking. It was almost psychic. He treated everybody as pieces on a board meant for his use. He'd know from his own movement how the defence was forming, and where the gaps were. In other words, he was the only imponderable, everybody else fell in predictable patterns around him."
Keshav Dutt, teammate

Born in 1905 as Dhyan Singh, he grew up playing with his friends on the dusty fields around his hometown Jhansi in Uttar Pradesh, using the branch of a palm tree as a hockey stick. At age 16, he followed his father Sameshwar Dutt Singh into the British Indian Army.

By now, he was already hooked to the game. He practised long and hard, often waiting for moonlit nights to illuminate his late-night practice sessions. When one of his army coaches called him Chand, meaning moon, Dhyan Singh became Dhyan Chand. He mastered his stick skills by running the ball along railway tracks and not allowing it to fall off.

But it was not just his dazzling stick work. Dhyan Chand was a team player with the finest hockey brain ever seen. As he sped around the field, he seemed to carry a map of the game in his head. He knew by instinct where to pass and to whom, he knew when to press forward, when to hold back, and when he could dash down the field dribbling the ball, slipping goals past the post while his opponents watched helplessly.

Dhyan Chand scored more than 1000 international goals in his 22-year career. A journalist who watched one of his matches, wrote, "This is not a game of hockey, but magic. Dhyan Chand is in fact the magician of hockey."

And that is how he is remembered even today, as the Magician of Hockey. The Wizard. The Pele of the Hockey World.

He was the key player of the Indian hockey team as they won three consecutive Olympic gold medals — 1928 in Amsterdam, 1932 in Los Angeles and 1936 in Berlin. In three Olympics, they conceded only three goals! With three more successive Olympic golds, India went on to dominate the sport of hockey.

Dhyan Chand's magical skills changed India's image as that of a poor, struggling colony of Great Britain. The world's attention was drawn to this all-powerful hockey team, this "typhoon out of the east" that just could not be defeated.

Now the undisputed champions of world hockey, India had arrived as a sporting power to be respected.

"Western recognition is nothing new for Dhyan Chand. Reports published in the 1930s make it clear that Dhyan Chand was an idol in the hockey world of Europe. Germany held him dear, calling their best hockey player 'the German Dhyan Chand'. At Prague a young lady insisted after the match on kissing India's hockey wizard, a demand that made him extremely uncomfortable. 'He is an angel,' she declared before kissing him."

Boria Mazumdar, sports journalist, 2015

"Often situations arise during a game when you are provoked. But you should exercise tolerance and show sportsmanship by putting restraint on your temper, and then the game will go on serenely as if nothing has happened. But if you take one false step, the field becomes an ugly scene. You lose your value…"

Dhyan Chand

"Hockey is a game of great skill. It calls for intelligence, keen eyes, powerful wrists, physical fitness and speed of mind and body. It also calls for great sportsmanship, tolerance and coolness. In short, hockey demands the best in you, both as a player and as a man."

XI.
OLYMPIADE
BERLIN
1936

LIGHTNING STICK

1905

Born to a Rajput family in Allahabad on 29 August, celebrated today as National Sports Day.

Due to his father's frequent transfers, his education stops after 6 years of schooling. The family settles in Jhansi. Dhyan's ambition as a boy is to be a wrestler.

1920s

In 1922, joins as a sepoy in the 1st Brahmans Regiment in Delhi, known for its hockey. Is trained in it by Subedar-Major Bale Tiwari.

Tiwari teaches him two important basics. One, not to get carried away with dribbling skills, to pass the ball when necessary. Two, to aim at the goal with accurate placement and push-strokes rather than mere power.

In 1924, at the final of the major Punjab Indian Infantry tournament in Jhelum, his side is losing. With four minutes to go, his commanding officer calls out, "Come on, Dhyan... Do something..." Dhyan scores three goals, and wins the match. They call him a "wizard"!

The Indian Army team tours Australia and New Zealand in 1926, in India's first hockey tournament abroad. He scores 100 of 192 goals in India's 18 wins out of 24 matches.

The newly formed Indian Hockey Federation (IHF) lobbies successfully to reintroduce hockey, after 1920, in the 1928 Amsterdam Olympics. Dhyan Chand's performance in the first Inter-Provincial tournament gets him into the Indian team.

In 1927, the team sails on the Kaiser-i-Hind from Mumbai, with only 3 people to see them off — the IHF president Major Burn-Murdoch, IHF vice-president C. E. Newham, and journalist S. Bhattacharjee.

In 11 pre-Olympic matches played in England, the Indians win 9 against local teams.

The English Hockey Association refuses to field the national team against India. It even withdraws from the Olympics, despite having won gold in two earlier Olympics — possibly not wanting to lose to its colony.

On 26 May 1928, India wins its first hockey gold at the Amsterdam Summer Olympics. The side is depleted with three sick. Dhyan Chand has high fever. The manager,

Pankaj Gupta, tells them, "Do or die" — and they beat the Dutch 3-0! Dhyan Chand scores 14 goals in 5 matches, the highest.

Cheering crowds now await them in Mumbai!

1930s

India wins hockey gold again at the 1932 Los Angeles Olympics beating Japan 11-1. Earlier they beat USA 24-1, a record at the time. A local paper calls the team a "typhoon out of the east". Dhyan Chand scores 12 goals overall.

In 1933, captains his home team Jhansi Heroes against the Calcutta Customs team to win the Beighton Cup. Calls it his best match ever.

Cricket legend Don Bradman meets him at Adelaide in 1935 and says "you score goals like runs"!

Captains India at the 1936 Berlin Olympics. India wins its third successive hockey gold, conceding only one goal in the entire tournament. Dhyan Chand bags 6.

The German papers are full of India's skill. One says the players "glided over turf as if it is a skating rink". Another runs the headline, "The Olympic complex now has a magic show too."

1947 – 48

The Asian Sports Association of East Africa invites India to a series, on condition that Dhyan Chand must come. He has begun to play fewer matches by now, but captains the international team one last time. Even at age 42, scores an impressive 61 goals in 22 matches.

Steps back from competitive hockey after this, having scored over 400 goals in his career.

1951

Honoured at the National Stadium, Delhi, with the launch of the Major Dhyan Chand Memorial Tournament.

1952

His autobiography *Goal!*, earlier serialised, is published by *Sport and Pastime*.

1956

Awarded the Padma Bhushan.

Retires from the army and starts coaching. Becomes Chief Hockey Coach at the National Institute of Sports, Patiala. The Dhyan Chand Award is now given to sportspeople who are not only great players but who continue to contribute to the sport after they retire.

दामोदर धर्मानन्द कोसांबी

D. D. KOSAMBI

1906–1966

At a time when 'interdisciplinary' was
an unfamiliar word, maverick scholar D. D. Kosambi flitted
comfortably back and forth between mathematics and
archaeology, statistics and Sanskrit. His independent and
remarkably creative mind used methods found in one subject to
ask questions of another. When he asked, "Why should there
be only one way of looking at history?" it took him to previously
unexplored aspects, revealing new dimensions
of Indian history and changing forever the way
it was researched and written.

STRANGE BUT TRUE. One of the most trailblazing books on Indian history was, in fact, written by a mathematician!

There was a time when Indian history was a yawn-inducing and seemingly never-ending list of kings and queens, saints, invasions, dates and political events. The authors were either colonialists or patriotic nationalists, and they focused on battle victories, sizes of kingdoms and the building of monuments.

In 1956 came a book called *An Introduction to the Study of Indian History.*

The author, D. D. Kosambi, was an eminent scholar — a mathematician. But that is not the only reason the book caused a stir. It was his approach to history that was unique. Instead of an excess of dates and names, there were questions. What sort of societies existed in earlier times? How did they produce food and other necessities? What sort of implements did they work with? Did everyone work? Who first thought of making coins? Why did people move from villages to cities? Why did Buddhism and Jainism start at around the same time and place? How was so much great Sanskrit literature written during the Gupta era?

And for the first time, the lives of the common people, their changing social and economic conditions were brought into the writing of Indian history. How had the author come upon such a unique outlook?

Maybe it had something to do with his background and education.

Damodar Dharmanand Kosambi was the son of a renowned scholar of Pali and Buddhism from Goa. When his father moved to the USA as visiting faculty at Harvard University, Damodar and his elder sister went with him.

By the time Kosambi himself graduated with distinction from Harvard University, he was already thought to be something of a prodigy. He studied mathematics and history and knew no less than a dozen languages, including Greek, Latin, Prakrit, Sanskrit, French, German, Russian, Spanish and Konkani! He was a fun-loving fitness fanatic, living in a spartan room with only a picture of Mahatma Gandhi as decoration and an array of books in different languages.

Later in life, he would talk of how much he owed to this wonderful education, the open environment with no limits to the subjects one chose to study.

"It was a memorable journey [from Bombay to Pune]. He had walked the entire route and knew every hill-top, stone and tree of consequence in terms of ethnographic and historical connections. His familiarity with the landscape was phenomenal. Those of us who were backing up our library research with fieldwork had to think again about the meaning of fieldwork and the co-relation of literary and tangible sources."
Romila Thapar, historian and Professor Emeritus, 2011

"Not that Kosambi himself was unaware of his acid tongue. He has himself recollected how, in his early boyhood, his grandmother would seat him upon her lap and put sugar into his mouth with a benediction that his words might be sweet. Kosambi wryly commented: 'Those who witnessed this charming, ridiculous, now forgotten observance feel, judging from the result, that she did not use enough sugar!'"
Ramkrishna Bhattacharya, academic writer, 2012

Moving back to India, he taught mathematics at Varanasi and Aligarh before finally moving to Fergusson College, Pune, where his father too had taught.

Things did not go very well, however. Kosambi liked to stretch the limits of his own knowledge and that of his students. He taught in a completely out-of-the-box style and had very little patience with an exam oriented education system. This did not go down well with the authorities and he was soon out of a job. He then worked at the Tata Institute of Fundamental Research. Here again, his forthrightness landed him in trouble when he said that India should really pursue solar power rather than the more expensive nuclear option!

All this while, Kosambi had been making a name for himself internationally in the fields of mathematics and genetics.

Working on a complex problem in statistics, he experimented with a hoard of antique punch-marked coins from Takshashila. Carefully sorting, analysing and weighing over 12,000 coins, Kosambi did not just solve his statistical problem but also ended up writing a scholarly paper on numismatics, the study of coins!

He now became curious about the kings or traders who had struck these coins, and began to look at old Sanskrit texts. Never one to do things casually, he spent five years reading and analysing the works of Bhartrihari, a fifth century CE grammarian and philosopher. Alongside, he did something no one had thought of doing before — he carefully examined the settings of these incredible Sanskrit texts to find information on the social and cultural life of ancient India!

He now urged historians to go beyond classical literature and involve themselves in archaeology, anthropology and sociology to find the material proof of their readings or theories. He himself did a lot of fieldwork, walking everywhere, picking up prehistoric tools and artefacts, exploring the Buddhist caves of the Western Ghats in great detail, interacting with tribal groups, and encouraging fieldworkers to "dig up people" rather than just collect artefacts.

Some of his ideas have now been challenged, but Kosambi's genius was the way he brought together his wide learning to ask the important question: What makes Indian civilisation uniquely Indian? Certainly not just dates and kings.

"The light-hearted sneer 'India has had some episodes, but no history' is used to justify lack of study, grasp, intelligence on the part of foreign writers about India's past. The considerations that follow will prove that it is precisely the episodes – lists of dynasties and kings, tales of war and battle spiced with anecdote, which fill school texts – that are missing from Indian records. Here, for the first time, we have to reconstruct a history without episodes, which means that it cannot be the same type of history as in the European tradition."

D. D. Kosambi

"Kosambi introduced a new method into historical scholarship, essentially by application of modern mathematics. By statistical study of the weights of the coins, Kosambi was able to establish the amount of time that had elapsed while they were in circulation and so set them in order to give some idea of their respective ages."

J. D. Bernal, scientist

Numismatics

the study
of coins

REWRITING HISTORY

1907

Born on 31 July in Goa. The family moves to Pune a few years later when his father starts teaching at Fergusson College. His early schooling is in Pune.

1918

In 1918, goes to Cambridge, Massachusetts, USA, with his father and sister. Becomes a friend of maths prodigy Norbert Wiener.

1920s

Finishes school in 1924 and comes back to India for college — but it proves difficult due to the different systems of education.

Joins Harvard University in 1926, majors in maths studying under George David Birkhoff. Takes diverse courses including many languages, and does brilliantly.

Graduates with high distinction in 1929. Made a member of the prestigious Phi Beta Kappa Society for outstanding students.

Returns to India as a professor of maths and German at Banaras Hindu University. Publishes his first research paper, 'Precessions of an Elliptica Orbit' in *Indian Journal of Physics*.

1930s

In 1931, moves to Aligarh Muslim University to teach maths at the call of French professor Andre Weil. Is popular with students because of his easy manner.

Produces more papers in maths — translates some himself for French, Italian and German journals.

Joins Fergusson College in Pune in 1933, where he teaches mathematics for 14 years. Fnds it difficult in the convention bound atmosphere. Light-heartedly calls his tenure "Rama's exile into the wilderness"!

In 1934, awarded the first Ramanujan Memorial Prize for maths. Also made a Foundation Fellow of C. V. Raman's Indian Academy of Science, Bengaluru.

1940s

To teach himself statistics, does a study of coins in 1940. His research is published much later in 1965 as 'Indian Numismatics' in *Scientific American*.

Fascinated by what coins show about the times, his interest in social sciences starts to grow. Begins to study Sanskrit classical literature to get a view of history from different angles and sources.

In 1944, writes a very successful paper on chromosome mapping, called the Kosambi Map Function, used widely by geneticists.

Publishes the first of his Sanskrit articles on Bhartrihari's work in 1945.

Begins a 5-year study of 400 ancient manuscripts to be able to do text-criticism of his works, in the process reviving over 50 forgotten Sanskrit poets. Says he has "fallen into Indology, as it were, through the roof"!

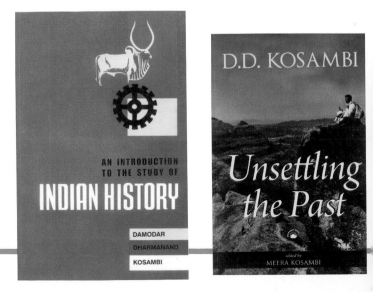

Starts to get politically active as a vocal Marxist.

Invited by scientist Homi Bhabha in 1946, to join as chair for mathematics at the newly established Tata Institute of Fundamental Research in Mumbai. Works there for 16 years.

Goes to England and the USA in 1948–49 as UNESCO fellow for research in electronic calculating machines. In London meets historian A. L. Basham, and they become good friends.

During his time in the USA, is visiting professor in path-geometry at Chicago. At the Institute for Advanced Study at Princeton, has long discussions with Einstein, Oppenheimer, Siegal, Neumann and other famous intellectuals of the day.

1950s

With the backdrop of the Cold War, joins the World Peace movement. In 1955, heads the Indian delegation to the World Peace Council in Helsinki. Begins to speak out against nuclear armament.

Invited by the Soviet Academy of Sciences to a conference on peaceful uses of atomic energy. China asks him to suggest statistical methods in food-crop forecasting and quality control in industry.

In 1956, publishes the path-breaking *An Introduction to the Study of Indian History*, which revolutionises the way ancient Indian history is seen, written and studied.

1960s

Appointed Scientist Emeritus in 1964 by the Council for Scientific and Industrial Research.

Founds an Archaeological Society at the National Defence Academy near Pune. Takes cadets hunting for megaliths and rock carvings, and discovers the Karsambla caves that have frescoes and carvings more beautiful than at Ajanta, though more damaged.

Dies suddenly on 29 June 1966. His fried Basham speaks in his obituary of the three things that most "filled his life to the exclusion of all others — ancient India, in all its aspects, mathematics and the preservation of peace".

હોમી જહાંગીર ભાભા

HOMI J. BHABHA

1909–1966

They called it Big Science when, during and after
World War II, governments of industrial nations scrambled
to fund giant projects and scientific institutions.
Returning from his studies in England, Homi Bhabha could see
that, approaching Independence, a developing India would also
need a strong science base. But where were the talent pools
to draw from? He took the initiative. State sanction, private
enterprise, his own vision… the brilliant experimental
scientist brought it all together to create top research
establishments and a nuclear programme
in one grand orchestration!

THE TATA TRUST was quite used to receiving appeals. Students wanted scholarships. Scientists needed research funds. But in 1944, there was a most unusual request. It came from a young physicist named Homi Jehangir Bhabha — he was not asking for a simple grant but a whole new institute!

This was Bhabha's rather bold proposal: "There is at the moment in India no big school of research in the fundamental problems of physics, both theoretical and experimental. There are, however, scattered all over India competent workers who are not doing as good work as they would do if brought together in one place under proper direction. It is absolutely in the interest of India to have a vigorous school of research in fundamental physics, for such a school forms the spearhead of research not only in less advanced branches of physics but also in problems of immediate practical application in industry."

It may have been the sheer conviction with which he wrote, or the fact that he was already an internationally renowned scientist, that made the Tata Trust agree to his proposal. The foundation was laid for what became two pillars of the Indian scientific establishment — the Tata Institute of Fundamental Research (TIFR), Mumbai, and the Atomic Energy Establishment, Trombay (later the Bhabha Atomic Research Centre or BARC).

It was the beginning of an extraordinary chapter in Indian scientific history.

Bhabha came from an affluent Parsi family of Mumbai. When he left to study mechanical engineering in Cambridge, England, his family hoped that their bright son would return to work as a metallurgist at the newly established Tata Iron and Steel Company in Jamshedpur. However, at Cambridge, he discovered his true passion was theoretical physics.

Nuclear physics was attracting the best minds in science at the time, and Bhabha went on to do a doctorate in it. His scientific papers were acclaimed in the academic world and he interacted with some of the most eminent physicists of the time, such as Neils Bohr, Paul Dirac and Walter Heitler.

In 1939, Bhabha was in India on a short holiday when World War II broke out. Rather than return to England, he took up a post at the Indian Institute

"When nuclear energy has been successfully applied for power production, in say a couple of decades from now, India will not have to look abroad for its experts but will find them ready at home."

Homi Bhabha, in his proposal to the Tata Trust to establish TIFR

"I am burning with a desire to do physics. I will and must do it sometime. It is my only ambition. I have no desire to be a `successful' man or the head of a big firm. There are intelligent people who like that and let them do it … It is no use saying to Beethoven `You must be a scientist for it is a great thing' when he did not care two hoots for science; or to Socrates `Be an engineer; it is work of intelligent man'. It is not in the nature of things. I therefore earnestly implore you to let me do physics."

Homi Bhabha, in a letter to his father from Cambridge

of Science where C. V. Raman was at the helm of affairs. This decision changed the course of scientific research in India.

Bhabha soon realised that what India's brainy scientific community needed was organised research and infrastructure of an international standard. Moreover, as Independence loomed closer, he was far-sighted enough to see that the new nation would need a firm scientific and technological base of its own. As ideas began to swirl in his head, he dashed off his famous proposal to the Tata Trust.

Even before the TIFR building could come up, Bhabha was already scouting for talent. Apart from nuclear physics and mathematics, he soon expanded to departments of molecular biology, radio astronomy and computer science. Bhabha firmly believed that scientific thinking was enhanced by the arts. So, with his refined taste, he supervised building designs to create modern institutes with plenty of open spaces, light and air. Gardens were planted with plants and trees that he often chose himself. Furniture was made from design magazines he brought back from Europe. Even tiny details like the canteen cutlery, menus and wall colours had his touch! A talented painter and musician himself, he acquired works of modern Indian artists like M. F. Husain, and arranged to have regular music concerts for his staff and faculty.

Post-Independence, he found a soulmate in Jawaharlal Nehru, who supported his visionary ideas and gave him the funding and liberty to run his institutions.

Homi Bhabha is best known today for guiding India's highly successful nuclear programme. India was short on uranium, so he came up with the bright idea of using its vast thorium reserves to extract power. This unusual move led to a unique three-stage programme which catapulted India into an elite set of nations that had managed to master this technology.

It is said that had Bhabha pursued his research career, he might have won a Nobel. Instead, he chose to build institutions that form the bedrock of India's atomic energy and nuclear programme. As the new nation began to find its feet, he ensured India was a scientific and nuclear power, able to use its own human and technological resources for industrial applications and national security.

The world began to sit up and take notice.

"Near his desk stood an enormous drawing board with huge printed plans pinned to it. It appeared that they were the first layout for the afforestation scheme and suggested gardens at Trombay. He spent many hours at night poring over these plans, trying to visualise in his mind's eye the setting of this new city which he had founded and built mostly below the tree-grown flanks of Trombay Hill ... It was typical of him that he could visualise the final shape of 'his' city only in its complete harmonious integration into the surrounding landscape."

Rudolf von Leyden, cartoonist and art critic, 1954

"Bhabha is a great lover of music, a gifted artist, a brilliant engineer and an outstanding scientist. He is the modern equivalent of Leonardo da Vinci."

C. V. Raman

Bhabha Scattering

Atoms for Peace Conference 1955

THORIUM

1909

Born on 30 October in Mumbai to a well-to-do and cultured Parsi family. His grandfather is an educationist, father a lawyer, industrialist Dorabji Tata his uncle. Grows up steeped in books, music and art.

1927

Joins Caius College, Cambridge University, England, to study mechanical engineering and realises that his calling is theoretical physics — but agrees to finish his course.

1930s

Gets a first class in mechanical sciences and then does his mathematics Tripos being taught by Paul Dirac, the Nobel Laureate.

Shifts to Cavendish Laboratory for his PhD in theoretical physics. Awarded several scholarships, including the Rouse Ball travelling studentship, which allow him to travel and work with famous European physicists such as Niels Bohr and Enrico Fermi.

Publishes a paper with a theory on electron-positron scattering, later named 'Bhabha Scattering' after him.

Also proposes a theory on cosmic ray shower formation with Walter Heitler. Wins him wide recognition as a talented physicist.

In 1939 World War II breaks out when he is in India, so he stays on.

1940s

In 1940, joins as a reader in theoretical physics at Indian Institute of Science, Bengaluru. Gets a grant from Dorabji Tata to start a Cosmic Ray Unit there. Is no longer interested in going back to England — feels responsible for doing things in India.

Elected a fellow of the Royal Society of London in 1941.

Awarded the Adams Prize in 1942 for his paper on 'The theory of the elementary particles and their interaction'.

Elected as fellow to the Indian Academy of Sciences.

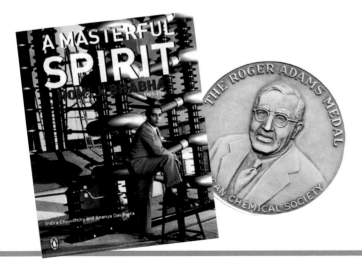

In 1944, writes to the Tata Trust for funding an institute devoted to cutting-edge science research. With a generous grant of one lakh rupees, the Tata Institute of Fundamental Research (TIFR), Mumbai, is inaugurated on 1 June 1945.

A few months after Independence, in 1948 writes to Nehru about setting up an Atomic Energy Commission (AEC). Nehru gives his full support and Bhabha becomes its first director.

Gives India's nuclear programme an early start, being very clear that it will be for peaceful purposes.

Visits a number of countries persuading talented Indian scientists to come and join the programme.

1950s

In 1951, becomes president of Indian Science Congress. Is also nominated for the Nobel Prize in Physics, though he does not win it.

In 1954, sets up the Atomic Energy Establishment at Trombay, near Mumbai, renamed Bhabha Atomic Research Centre (BARC) in 1966.

Becomes secretary to the Government of India in the Department of Atomic Energy.

Awarded the Padma Bhushan in 1954.

Is president of the first United Nations Conference on Peaceful Uses of Atomic Energy in Geneva in 1955.

1960s

In 1960, is made president, until 1963, of the International Union of Pure and Applied Physics.

As part of the Scientific Advisory Committee to the government, in 1962 initiates plans for a space research programme, later helmed by Vikram Sarabhai.

Construction of India's first atomic power station begins in Tarapur in 1963.

Dies suddenly in a mysterious plane crash near Mont Blanc in Switzerland in 1966, surrounding which are many conspiracy theories. He once prophetically said, "I cannot increase the content of life by increasing its duration, I will increase it by increasing its intensity."

ദാക്ഷായണി വേലായുധൻ

DAKSHAYANI VELAYUDHAN

1912–1978

Going to school, getting a college degree
and keeping the upper body covered do not sound
like revolutionary activities. For Dakshayani Velayudhan, they were.
In early 20th century Kerala, they were outright challenges to established
caste rules, and the consequences were hostility and rejection.
Undaunted, the courageous girl went on to find her voice, confronting
injustice and stringing together a series of firsts for a woman from her
Pulaya community. She carried her questioning right into the hall
of the Constituent Assembly, where she was the only
female Dalit, seeking social justice so others
like her could walk tall.

DON'T! NO! CAN'T! Shouldn't! Mustn't!

Just like most of us, Dakshayani heard those words very often while growing up. But unlike most of us, they were not used only to stop her from being naughty or grabbing her brother's share of payasam.

What else was not allowed?

Almost everything, as it turns out.

At the turn of the 20th century, being born into the Pulaya community in Kochi, Kerala, meant a life full of cruel discrimination. Rigid caste rules at the time forbade the people of this Dalit community a lot of things. No cutting hair. No clothes on the upper body — so most women covered themselves with grass or bead necklaces. No attending school, going to markets or even walking on public roads. They had to walk with their heads bowed all the time, calling out every few steps to warn others of their 'polluting' presence. If they dared to come within a few paces of upper caste people, even by accident, or look up as they passed by, the punishment was severe.

Luckily for Dakshayani Velayudhan, she was born at a time when social protests at these inhumane rules had begun — although just about.

The maharaja of Kochi had forbidden any gathering of Dalits on his land. So some members of the community, including Dakshayani's brothers and uncles, decided to meet on water! They strung together a row of boats on the backwaters. On those wobbly catamarans, a historic meeting took place where they formed the Pulaya Mahajana Sabha, an organisation to fight for their rights.

But when Dakshayani's brothers cut their hair and began to wear shirts, people threw stones at them in the streets. Dakshayani herself was mocked for her name, considered a bit too grand for a Pulaya girl. In reply, her strong willed mother put her in a dress and sent her to a free government school.

It was not easy for the little girl to take a ferry and walk almost two hours back and forth. But Dakshayani was unstoppable. And she was smart. She won a government scholarship and went on to do a degree in chemistry, becoming the

"At five feet, [Dakshayani] Velayudhan was 'unassuming and serious' and walked with a slight slouch, [her daughter] Meera says. It came during the early years in Mulavukad, when she and others from her community walked with their head down and backs hunched. But the value of standing tall, head held high and striving in the face of great adversity was never lost on her. Meera remembers an innocuous incident, while studying at night: 'I was preparing for an exam, possibly all slouched, with a flask of coffee to keep awake. When she saw me sitting like that, she patted me on the back and said, sit straight.'"
Sanchari Pal, journalist, 2018

first Dalit woman to earn a college degree. Following a teacher's training course in Chennai, she went back to Kerala to work in a government school.

Despite all her achievements, Dakshayani had to fight extreme prejudice almost every day of her life. Her chemistry professor would not allow her to touch the lab equipment for fear of contamination — Dakshayani could only observe experiments from afar. Later, as a teacher herself with official accommodation provided to her, she was not allowed to draw water from the common well as she was considered unclean. Although her mother, who had converted to Christianity by then, was allowed to draw the water for her!

The oppression took its toll, but Dakshayani was not defeated.

She began to use her hard won education and her personal experiences of injustice to question social prejudices and discrimination, now interacting and often arguing even with Gandhi and Ambedkar. At her marriage to the Dalit leader R. K. Velayudhan, Gandhi and his wife Kasturba were the witnesses and the officiating priest was a leper. She was nominated to the Cochin Legislative Council where she was an outspoken member, criticising the inhumanity of untouchability and fighting for the rights of Dalits.

In 1946, Dakshayani stepped onto the national stage. She was appointed a member of the Constituent Assembly, the organisation that drafted the Indian Constitution. By now, she had become a fearless speaker, able to hold her own even when her ideas differed from those of Gandhi and Ambedkar. She told the council in no uncertain terms that caste discrimination could end not merely by enforcing rules but by bringing about a change in people's attitudes. She spoke so boldly that the chairman was often afraid of stopping her even when she ran over the time limit!

Dakshayani Velayudhan turned her own bitter experiences into a fight for the rights of other oppressed people.

Along the way, she exploded many myths about what a poor, so-called untouchable girl could achieve. Her voice lives on in the Constitution of India.

"I submit that a Constituent Assembly not only frames a Constitution but also gives the people a new framework for life ... what we want is not all kinds of safeguards. It is the moral safeguards that give us real protection ... what we want is the immediate removal of our social disabilities. Our freedom can be obtained only from Indians and not only from the British Government."

Dakshayani Velayudhan

"I was always proud of my background, confident of my abilities and never felt downtrodden ... When I started my menstruation, I was nine, during holidays, she sketched and explained what was happening to the body and asked my father to get some sanitary pads to take to school."

Meera Velaudhan, policy analyst and Dakshayani's daughter, about her mother

"As long as the Scheduled Castes, or the Harijans or by whatever name they may be called, are economic slaves of other people, there is no meaning demanding either separate electorates or joint electorates or any other kind of electorates with this kind of percentage."

ഭരണഘടന

CONSTITUTION

FIRST AMONG EQUALS

1912

Born on 4 July in Mulavukad, an island village in Ernakulam, Kerala. The Pulaya community she belongs to is one of the earliest inhabitants of Kerala — severely discriminated against and treated as untouchables.

Social change began with the Channar revolt and the work of Ayyankali and Sree Narayana Guru. Dakshayani's family has been active in the reform movement.

1913

The Kochi maharaja forbids Pulayas to hold meetings "on my land", so they hold the Kayal Sammelanam, meaning 'meeting on the backwaters', on rafts and boats. Members of her family attend.

1918

Among the first generation in her community to be educated, she starts going to St Mary's School. She is the first Pulaya girl to start covering her upper body, and also the first to pass the ESLC exam.

1935

Graduates from Maharaja's College, Ernakulam, the only girl in the science department. Becomes the first female Dalit in India to finish college.

Goes on to do a teacher's training course in Chennai and teaches till 1945 in Thrissur and Tripunithura.

1940s

In 1940, marries Raman Kelan Velayudhan, a Dalit leader, at Sevagram in Wardha in Gandhi's presence.

Soon after, becomes editor of Gandhi Era Publications in Chennai.

Gets herself nominated to the Cochin Legislative Council in 1945, to be a voice for her community. Gives her first, hard-hitting, speech in English, calling untouchability inhuman. Says that as long as it is practised, 'Harijan' is as meaningless as referring to dogs as 'Napoleon'.

In 1946, the Constituent Assembly is formed. Of 389 members only 15 are women — many privileged, like Vijayalakshmi Pandit, Sarojini Naidu and Rajkumari Amrit Kaur, and only one Dalit — 34-year-old Dakshayani.

She becomes known for asking difficult questions and for her fiery, radical speeches. Supports Ambedkar's insistence on social equality for all.

Becomes editor of *The Common Man*, Chennai.

In a debate in the Assembly in 1948, says forcefully that "we cannot expect a Constitution without relating to untouchability". Calls for "proper propaganda done by both the Central and Provincial Governments".

DAKSHAYANI VELAYUDHAN

1912 - 1978

Dakshayani Velayudhan (1912-1978), the first Dalit woman in the Constituent Assembly of India.

- #WomensPolitical EmpowermentDay

"There were many firsts in Dakshayani's life... The first Dalit girl to attend school wearing an upper cloth, [and] the first Dalit woman graduate in India ...there were many assertions too – of not walking with shoulders bent or not making way for upper castes while walking on the road."

- Meera Velayudhan, her daughter.

Passes away in 1978, having shattered the ceilings imposed by both caste and gender. Forty years later, in 2019, the Dakshayani Velayudhan Award is instituted by the Kerala government for women who contribute to empowering other women in the state.

1950s

On 26 January 1950, the Constitution comes into effect. Till general elections are held, the Constituent Assembly becomes the Provisional Parliament, in which Dakshayani continues as a member from the Congress.

Her husband too becomes a member of the Provisional Parliament in 1952, from the Socialist Party, making them possibly the first Dalit parliamentarian couple.

1970s

Contests for the Lok Sabha elections in 1971 from the Adoor constituency, but loses.

In 1977, organises a national conference for Dalit women, with other Ambedkarites. Over 200 women attend. Sets up the Mahila Jagriti Parishad that begins to work with sweeper women from the slums in South Delhi, to provide literacy and training for other kinds of employment.

مقبول فدا حسین

M. F. HUSAIN

1915–2011

Once a struggling painter of film hoardings,
he went on to become a superstar in the world of art,
selling his works for millions. M. F. Husain's inspirations came from
the folk heart of his country, its mythology and people, and his own
composite religious and cultural background. So, while his
free-spirited abstracts were displayed in chic art galleries,
they made as much sense to the common man. He left his own
distinctive imprint on the evolving contemporary art
of modern India, becoming one of its most
internationally recognised artists.

AT A FAMOUS LONDON MUSEUM, beautiful modern art paintings are on display. One of them is called 'Indian Households'. Three separate panels depict everyday scenes from the lives of a Muslim, a Hindu and a Sikh family. If you peer very closely at the first of these panels, you will see a little boy hiding under a bed, drawing a horse. That rather forlorn figure is a self-portrait of one of India's most celebrated artists as a boy.

Maqbool Fida Husain was born in Pandharpur, Maharashtra, losing his mother before he turned two. His father remarried and moved to Indore. In a house full of siblings, no one paid much attention to the young boy. He took to wandering the streets with his friends after school — hanging out at crowded marketplaces, observing people and hearing their stories. He watched the rituals at the local temple, gazed in awe at the white horses of the Muharram procession, and listened with rapt attention when his Hindu friend told him stories from the epics. Marvelling at images, colour and light, he felt an inner urge to draw or paint what he saw. Paints and brushes would have been a luxury, so he taught himself how to draw by tracing the covers of magazines. His talent was obvious, but plans to go to art school in Mumbai were shelved when his father lost his job.

A determined Husain, around 18 now, moved to Mumbai anyway. He got work painting huge, colourful film hoardings. But he continued with his art, waking up at four to paint before heading off to work. He sold his first painting for the grand sum of ten rupees. Not a lot of money, but a great boost to his confidence. To make ends meet, he also began to design and make toys and furniture.

The mid-1940s brimmed with talk of an independent India — secular, democratic, socially just, forward in outlook. A few artists thought the time had come to bring fresh ideas into the world of art too. They formed the Progressive Artists' Group and Husain was asked to join them. Together, they explored modern styles, materials and subjects to represent the new India. Their paintings were more abstract. Figures were broken up, moved around, shown from different angles, mashed together. Some viewers found these difficult to understand but they knew they were looking at something original and exciting and full of emotion. It was a language of art for a nation that was finding itself — themes and ideas rooted in Indian tradition but with contemporary techniques.

"Maqbool Fida Husain has dominated the Indian art scene for 60 years, his detractors as much in awe of him as his devotees. To watch him cover a vast canvas is awe-inspiring. Drawing in big black lines he then fills [in] with thick swathes of pigment, tackling colour, light and shade simultaneously as the picture emerges..."
Anjoli Ela Menon, artist, 2001

"Husain's art was celebratory ... 'Dancing, singing, joy are central to our culture. Sentiments are our strength,' he said ... Husain succeeded in living life on his terms and painting it on his terms. He may have apologised to whoever chose to be offended by his work, but that was because fighting didn't interest him. Faced with a blank canvas, he marked it exactly as he wanted. In that gesture lay his freedom, and his courage, as an artist."
Girish Shahane, art critic, 2012

Husain now came into his element. In all his years of struggle as a painter of hoardings, he had picked up important skills. Powerful lines, vivid colour, the ability to work quickly yet achieve great balance in his work. What made him different was his strong connect to the common folk of India. He painted ordinary people — potters and village women standing in urban backgrounds. He painted scenes from the *Ramayana* and *Mahabharata*, gods and goddesses, and the huge white horses of his childhood memories, all in a modern style.

And he chronicled India's life — the British Raj, Independence, a cyclone in Andhra Pradesh, the massacre in Assam, the assassination of Indira Gandhi. He painted Mother Teresa, and sports and film stars including his favourite muse, the actress Madhuri Dixit. To him, India was a "museum without walls" in which people lived in harmony regardless of their religion or culture. He called himself a folk painter because he did not paint in remote studios but wherever he happened to be, often on the floors of hotel rooms.

Husain believed modern art techniques were rooted not in Western civilisation, but in the tribal and folk traditions of India. Once, he took 80 of his paintings on a bullock cart to a village in Andhra Pradesh. The villagers were not at all surprised by the style where head, limbs and torso of the gods and goddesses were not where you would normally expect them to be! They understood the abstract style by instinct for that was how they too painted. As Husain said, "You put an orange spot on a stone and the people will know it is Hanuman."

He created more than 40,000 works of art. His quirky nature saw him walk barefoot, even to parliament! But he was a striking figure with his neat grey beard, well cut suits, and a walking stick which was in fact a very long paintbrush. Playful and creative, his phone ringtone was a recording of a cock crowing back in his hometown of Pandharpur! Travelling the world as India's most well known modern artist, he never forgot his roots. Even in his last years, forced into exile by people who could not understand his work, he talked of sneaking back to India just to have a cup of chai at the local tea stall.

Husain never really got over the loss of his mother. He once said that his art was an outpouring in search of a mother figure. It is not hard to see the longing in the little boy tucked under a bed, drawing his heart out.

"In the end, gloom did cast its shadow on him, when self-appointed custodians of culture took umbrage at a Muslim's brush depicting Hindu divinities in ways beyond their creative comprehension. But by then the boy from Pandharpur was already a legend: he had nothing to prove any more, and if at all a loss was incurred, it was not by him but by an entire nation."

Manu S. Pillai, historian and writer, 2018

"I put six canvases on the floor – they were of different sizes. One may be very violent, another very lyrical ... this was all to demonstrate that the human mind can work simultaneously on different levels, you have to develop. And in a split second, you can move from one mood to another. That is how I did those six paintings. What happened? In the end, there were two paintings which didn't work, they were a flop. This is the mystery of creation, that even after painting for 40 years, 50 years, still sometimes you can miss.

This is the mystery which fascinates everyone. If you are not shy of your weaknesses, then you have no inhibitions."

M. F. Husain

PROGRESSIVE ARTISTS' GROUP

BAREFOOT AND FREE

1915

Born on a date no one really remembers. He himself chooses 17 September 1917 "because I liked the sound of September". Later, he decides there are too many 's' sounds in it, so changes the year to 1915!

Belongs to a Sulaymani Bohra family, living in the temple town of Pandharpur in Maharashtra. Loses his mother when he is about one and a half years old. His father remarries and they move to Indore.

As a child, loves calligraphy, poetry and painting, and taking pictures with the Agfa camera box his father gifts him. Paints portraits from age 11.

1930s

Determined to be a painter, he moves to Mumbai. Gets a job painting film hoardings. Once he has to do a 40-foot cutout of an actress overnight, so he spreads the canvas on the road after the last tram goes and finishes before the first tram comes next morning!

His maiden show in 1934 gets plenty of criticism. But he manages to sell a watercolour for ten rupees.

Joins the prestigious JJ School of Art, Mumbai, in 1935.

1940s

After marriage and children, starts working at Fantasy Furniture Shop designing very imaginative furniture and wooden toys — shows early signs of his signature style.

Gets in the limelight in 1946 when his oil painting 'Sunehra Sansar' wins a prize at the Bombay Art Society exhibition.

The Progressive Artists' Group (PAG) is formed in 1947 with F. N. Souza, S. H. Raza, K. H. Ara, H. A. Gade and S. K. Bakre as members. Souza is impressed by Husain's work and asks him to join. The PAG artists do not want to paint objects as seen, but express their feelings about what they see. It is a renaissance movement in Indian art.

1950s

Holds his first solo exhibition in Zurich in 1952.

Goes on a barefoot tour across Europe. Sees the works of Pablo Picasso and Henri Matisse, particularly influenced by Paul Klee. But is conscious that his own art must be Indian.

In 1955, wins first prize at Lalit Kala Akademi's National Exhibition of Art for 'Zameen'.

In 1959, gets the International Biennale Award in Tokyo.

1967

Turns filmmaker. His debut film, a documentary called *Through the Eyes of a Painter* wins a National Film Award, as well as the Golden Bear at the Berlin Film Festival in the Short Film category.

1971

Special invitee along with Pablo Picasso to the Bienal de Sao Paulo art show in Brazil.

1986

Nominated to the Rajya Sabha. Attends sessions for 6 years without ever speaking, but sketching — "because a painter's job is to observe," he says.

1990s

Awarded the Padma Vibhushan in 1991.

In 1992, along with architect Balkrishna Doshi, starts constructing the underground cave art gallery known as Amdavad ni Gufa in Ahmedabad. It holds his largest painting, the 100-foot long 'Sheshnag'.

In 1996, Hindi magazine *Vichar Mimansa* publishes his paintings of Hindu goddesses from the 1970s and starts off a controversy fuelled by extreme Hindu groups. Criminal complaints are filed accusing him of hurting Hindu sentiments. His house and works are vandalised.

2000s

Produces and directs the film *Gaja Gamini* in 2000, his ode to womanhood, starring Madhuri Dixit.

Radical Hindu groups again create a furore in 2006 over his painting 'Mother India'. "It's not a lot of people," he says about them. "They have never stopped me working, they never will of course." But he is forced to leave India for good, spending time between Doha and London.

In 2008, Christie's sells his painting 'Battle of Ganga and Jamuna: Mahabharata 12' for a record 1.6 million dollars.

Qatar confers citizenship on him in 2010.

Undertakes to make 32 large-scale paintings on Indian civilisation but completes only 8 before he dies in 2011.

Towards the end he says, "For centuries India has accomodated all faiths. It was a unique composite culture. But there are forces within every culture that want to turn away from that. To purify things. I've wanted to celebrate this composite culture…"

بیگم اختر
BEGUM AKHTAR

1914–1974

The feudal-era patronage of music,
with private mehfils and singing courtesans was changing.
New media of records and radio, as also public concerts, were
reaching a wider audience. Hindustani classical ragas were
evolving lighter, more popular, forms. Among all the other gifted
singers of the time, Begum Akhtar's husky voice captivated with
her thumris and dadras. And her ghazals! Enriching them with
raga based melody, adapting contemporary Urdu poetry,
raising the stature of the female singer to that of a
shayar, or poet, she took the ghazal to levels
never known before.

AT A FUND-RAISING CONCERT in Kolkata, there was panic backstage. None of the artists set to perform had turned up, and the audience was getting restless! Ustad Ata Mohammed Khan, a respected classical singer, stepped in. He suggested a student of his sing a few ghazals to keep the audience entertained till the main performers arrived. A very young Akhtari walked nervously onto stage. She had never sung in front of such a large crowd. But from the moment she began in her deep, rich, emotion laden voice, everyone was spellbound.

That evening, the legend of Akhtari Bai Faizabadi was born.

People said that Akhtari Bai had a special quality to her voice, a kind of sadness that gave her ghazals a haunting, unforgettable quality. Perhaps that came from a childhood of sorrow, loss and plenty of drama. Her affluent father disowned them before she and her twin sister Anwari were even born. Leaving Lucknow for Faizabad, her mother struggled to bring them up on her own. When the twins were about four, Anwari tragically died, it was said from eating poisoned sweets. Akhtari was so traumatised that she never spoke of the incident again. Soon after, their house burned down and they had to move yet again.

Akhtari's mother, Mushtari Begum, was a well known courtesan-singer. Recognising that her spirited daughter had a fine voice, she decided to have her learn from the best possible teacher. After training her for a while, Ustad Ata Mohammed Khan realised that Akhtari's expressive voice was better suited to the more evocative ghazals, dadras and thumris, rather than formal khayals.

After moving to Kolkata in the 1930s, she and her mother had fallen on hard times. This was probably why Akhtari started to accept offers to act on stage despite her guru's disapproval. Her beauty and singing talent landed her roles in the movies too, and she acted and sang in nine films.

With all the attention from her solo concert, she also signed a deal with the Megaphone Company to record professionally as Akhtari Bai Faizabadi. When her seventh 78 rpm record released with the ghazal 'Deewana banana hai toh deewana bana de…' she was a celebrity! Her legions of fans were mesmerised by her husky, melodious voice. They raved about the unique 'patti'

"Through Begum Akhtar's music, millions of people have been led unawares to an understanding of Indian classical music and Urdu poetry which they on their own would never have thought of acquiring."

"Rasoolan Bai was like vintage brandy – deep and mellow. Siddheshwari Devi was like a bird of paradise who threw her heart and soul into heaven with much energy and passion. Begum Akhtar's technique was much subtler; you never associated her music with effort."
Sheila Dhar, singer and writer

"Her methods were unorthodox. There were no fixed hours … She would sing for hours together and told me to learn by listening. Sometimes if I got a note wrong she would threaten to throw the harmonium at me! And yet she was the most loving, generous ustad one could have."
Shanti Hiranand, Begum Akhtar's first disciple

or crack in her voice on the higher notes, which would have been frowned upon in any other singer. They waited eagerly for her next record.

Then, quite abruptly, Akhtari gave it all up and went back to further her music, training under Ustad Abdul Wahid Khan. Her songs now had a stronger classical base. Once again, she became a much sought after performer, being wooed by royalty from Hyderabad, Kashmir, Darbhanga and Rampur to sing in their courts.

When she was 30, Akhtari met and married a successful lawyer from Lucknow and stopped singing altogether. Now Begum Abbasi, she gave herself up to her new responsibilities. It is said that the lull in her career was because her husband's family did not consider it respectable for her to perform in public. But when her beloved mother died, Akhtari became so mad with grief that the doctors suggested she start singing again to recover from deep depression.

By now, things had changed in India. Post-Independence, the old feudal ways of courts and kings had ended. There were no longer patrons to support artists and their carefully cultivated forms of music. The government stepped in, and radio was the new way to promote culture. All India Radio became her saviour — she could perform, yet stay away from the public gaze. She now came to be known as Begum Akhtar.

By the 1960s, she was at the height of her popularity, invited to musical conferences all over India and concert tours abroad. Both she and her husband had a deep interest in Urdu poetry. Their home became the hub of poets and musicians. Well known Urdu poets presented their poems to use as ghazals. Unknown poets competed with each other for Begum Akhtar's attention and were honoured when she used their couplets. She took on a few students and was known as a strict but generous teacher.

Through her simplicity and the way she revealed her soul or 'taseer' in her voice, she enthralled a receptive new nationwide audience. To the rich and intricate musical legacy of the ghazal, thumri and dadra, which had once been heard by only a select few, Begum Akhtar added her own inimitable flourish, leaving her signature on them for posterity.

"She had little formal education but a highly developed aesthetic sense which would be the envy of the most sophisticated, well-read members of the privileged class. She also brought to the fore poets like Shakeel Badayuni, who wrote about everyday emotions ... and promoted younger, more populist poets ... She had the ability to dignify and elevate relatively lesser-known poetry and bring out the nuances of seemingly ordinary verse that the lay reader was most likely to miss."

Partha Chatterjee, scholar and culture critic, 2009

"Radio proved to be the medium which provided initial anonymity and a respectable platform to perform ... In the post-Independence era, in the process of proclaiming a national identity, it became radio's mandate to promote the national culture."

The Begum Akhtar Centenary Commemoration Project, IGNCA

A LIFETIME
COMES A PICTURE

Such Heart-Warming
Heart-Winning
Sincerity ......
Such Rich Humour
Such Deep Human
Understanding
As You Will Find In
Magnificent Master

Starring:
CHANDRAMOHA
SHAIKH MUKHTA
SITAR
AKHTARI FAIZA
ASHRAF KHA

NATIONAL'S GLORIOUS OFFERING THE NATION!

ROTI

PRODUCED &
DIRECTED BY
MEHBOOB

AKHTARI BAI FAIZABADI

1914

Born on 7 October in Faizabad, Uttar Pradesh.

1920s–30s

Loves music and watching nautanki theatre. At age 7, is fascinated by the singing of Chandra Bai in a touring theatre group. Begins learning Hindustani classical singing from Ustad Imdad Khan.

Moves to Gaya with her mother. Trains now under Ustad Ata Mohammed Khan of the Patiala gharana. Shifts focus from classical khayal to the lighter thumri, dadra and ghazal.

Gives her first performance aged around 12.

Her mother and ustad decide they should move to Kolkata, a big city with more opportunity.

Catches attention when she sings at a charity concert (at which shehnai player Bismillah Khan also debuts).

The Megaphone Company signs her up for several records. She is one of the early artists in the gramophone era — talented courtesans such as Gauhar Jaan have already taken the lead in adapting to this new technology.

Akhtari acts in a lead role for an Urdu play at the Corinthian Theatre. Gives up rigorous music training for lack of time but continues performing at gatherings.

Begins to act and sing in films. The first, *Ek Din Ka Badshah*, is released in 1933. She shifts to Mumbai and is known as Miss Akhtari Bai Filmstar.

In the late 1930s, gives up films and returns to serious classical music, learning from Ustad Abdul Wahid Khan of the Kirana gharana. Develops into a sought after singer.

1940s

In 1942, stars in the film *Roti*, directed by the famous filmmaker Mehboob Khan.

In 1945, marries Ishtiaq Ahmed Abbasi, the nawab of Kakori and a well known barrister in Lucknow. Gives up singing in public.

A connoisseur of Urdu poetry, Abbasi introduces her to the work of poets such as Meer Taqi Meer, Mirza Ghalib, Faiz Ahmed Faiz, Momin, Jigar Moradabadi... This enhances her understanding of Urdu poetry and the way she sings ghazals.

In 1948, does a one-off recording with All India Radio (AIR), Lucknow. Now takes the name Begum Akhtar for her singing — a persona distinct from Begum Abbasi.

1950s

Her mother and constant companion, Mushtari Bai, passes away in 1951. Akhtari is hysterical with grief. To help her recover, her family agrees to let her return to public performances.

Makes a comeback the same year at the Shankar Lal Festival in Delhi.

Takes on some students.

Her final film *Jalsaghar* releases in 1958, in which director Satyajit Ray convinces her to do a cameo.

1960s–70s

Is now an A-grade artist of All India Radio and sings at major concerts or 'conferences' all over India. These are organised post-Independence to popularise classical music among the public.

Also performs in Afghanistan, Pakistan and the USSR.

In 1961, her recital at the All Bengal Music Conference is considered iconic in her career.

At the Ghalib Centenary celebrations, she releases a long-playing record of Mirza Ghalib's ghazals.

Awarded the Padma Shri in 1968. The Padma Bushan comes after her death, in 1975.

Given the Sangeet Natak Akademi Award in 1972.

Dies of a heart attack after a scintillating concert at Ahmedabad in 1974.

Leaves behind almost 400 songs to her credit. One of her most distinctive features is the crack in her voice in the higher octave — a flaw she elegantly turns into her charm. Shehnai maestro Bismillah Khan says he would wait for it: "Wah! This is what I wanted to hear!"

HITS OF EGUM AKHTAR

எம். எஸ். சுப்புலட்சுமி

M. S. SUBBULAKSHMI

1916–2004

A singing voice so clear and lustrous,
almost divine... M. S. Subbulakshmi brought something
more than technical perfection. It was a mystique, creating a
mood that filled the soul of the audience. Along with other singers
like D. K. Pattammal and M. L. Vasanthakumari, she breached the
bastion of male dominance in the Carnatic concert circuit.
Then, through films, records and live performances,
her music bridged divides to reach a national audience.
And from there, the world, to give it a rare taste of
Carnatic music, leaving it enthralled.

SEPTEMBER 1947. The family of noted singer, M. S. Subbulakshmi has an urgent phone call. Will she be able to sing Gandhi's favourite Meera bhajan at a concert in Delhi? The answer is hesitant. MS Amma can't travel at this time. Besides, she doesn't know the song. Perhaps they should request another singer. But Gandhi is firm: "I would rather Subbulakshmi *spoke* the bhajan than anyone else sing it!" Overnight, after some hurried practice, a tape with 'Hari tuma haro' is sent to Delhi just in time for Bapu's birthday.

A few months later, on 30 January 1948, a sombre announcement on All India Radio says Mahatma Gandhi has been assassinated. And then, the same tape of 'Hari tuma haro' comes on. Listening in faraway Chennai, Subbulakshmi breaks down in tears.

MS, as she came to be known, was destined to be a musician. She was born into a family of devadasis — women who were dedicated to temples to devote their lives to music and dance as offerings to the deity. Her great-grandmother was a famed dancer who was said to have performed for the viceroy in 1886, her grandmother was a violinist, and her mother a talented veena player.

She and her two siblings grew up in a modest house in Madurai, filled with the sound of music as their mother practised and performed. MS was taught to play the veena and mridangam but it was clear from the start that her real talent lay in her extraordinary voice. As a ten-year-old, she and her mother cut a gramophone record together — 'Maragatha vadivum'. Her resonant voice with its startling pitch and range turned MS into a singing sensation.

Later, she would laugh recalling how she would be dragged from her mud-pie making sessions with her siblings when important visitors came to hear her sing! The shy girl was styled by her mother in puff-sleeved blouses, pinned half-sarees, and a tight braid that tried to bring her corkscrew curls under control with a banana reed hair tie or a mismatched ribbon.

The family moved to Chennai, the centre of music sabhas. In those days, the world of Carnatic music was a conservative one where women simply did not perform on stage. But it was clear that MS had something exceptional. Experts were stunned by her poise, her technical skill and her pitch perfect

"The event [a wedding] had drawn a galaxy of artists ... The next day, in the midst of this starry assembly, Dakshinamurti Pillai suddenly smote his head ... 'How will you save your throats for a lifetime if you engage in vocal gymnastics? Leave all that to us drummers. Singers must emphasise the raga and the bhava so that you preserve your voice and let it gain in timbre. That little girl there, she knows this already. Didn't we hear her yesterday?'"
Gowri Ramnarayan, writer, about 12-year-old MS, 2004

"Coming from the Devadasi community, the way MS has fought her disadvantaged situation is remarkable ... The conservative Carnatic music cabal, the major dominance of the man and active suppression of the woman; and if MS fought all this some 70 years ago, it is certainly not a small thing."
From a review of T. J. S. George's book, *MS: A Life in Music* in *The Hindu*, 2004

voice. But there was something more — MS sang with a deep emotion that added a spiritual quality to her songs.

When she married Tyagaraja Sadasivam, he recognised her special talent and began to direct her performances. Now, apart from traditional Carnatic music, she sang bhajans and patriotic songs in ten different languages to reach a wider audience. To many in the north of India, this was their first introduction to Carnatic music. All the money from her concerts went to charities for social, religious and nationalist causes. Prominent leaders of the freedom struggle — Gandhi, Nehru and C. Rajagopalachari — attended her concerts.

Sadasivam also introduced MS to cinema. She acted in four movies, drawing in audiences with her serene beauty and flawless singing. But it was in her role of Meera, the queen-turned-poet and singer, that she mesmerised the entire nation. It seemed that she was, like Meera herself, a saint whose songs were a form of devotion to god. At the Delhi premiere of the Hindi remake, Sarojini Naidu introduced the film, while Lord and Lady Mountbatten along with Jawaharlal Nehru welcomed the invitees.

To India, MS had become Meera. She was now a household name everywhere. But none of this fame affected her. When she sang, she still had an inner radiance that seemed to spread through the audience.

With her distinctive rich kanjeevaram sarees, flashing diamond nose studs and fresh flowers in her hair, MS lit up the world of classical music. Musicians from all styles praised her supreme skill — Bade Ghulam Ali Khan, Roshanara Begum, Pandit Ravi Shankar and Pandit Jasraj were all admirers.

Having introduced Carnatic music to the rest of India, she then went on to the world stage, performing at the Edinburgh Music Festival and at Carnegie Hall. Audiences who could not understand a word she sang, sat spellbound through her performances. She became the first Indian musician to perform at the United Nations General Assembly. In a memorable finale, she sang 'Maitreem bhajata', a prayer specially written by the Kanchi Paramacharya, calling for an end to warfare and for friendship among nations. It received a standing ovation.

That shy girl from Madurai had become the voice of India.

"The difference between a good musician and a great musician is the skill of communication. You may have all the technical skills in the book but unless you are in sync with the audience in front of you all your skills are a waste. M. S. Subbulakshmi was one of the greatest communicators."

T. M. Krishna, Carnatic vocalist

"MS is of historical importance. Not because of the recognition she has earned, or because of the titles she has got. Not even that she is the best in the Carnatic music field. But MS ... has achieved something very different ... She was never a fighter like Balasaraswati. But in her own quiet way, non-fighting way, she broke those [male] barriers. She was the first woman to be the chairperson of the Music Academy. Who [else] can tell you that story?"

T. J. S. George, writer and biographer, 2004

Meera (1945)

SAKUNTALAI SONGS

KOKILAGANA ISAIVANI
M.S. SUBBULKSHMI

"HIS MASTER'S VOICE"

MS SUBBULAKSHMI

THE MS MYSTIQUE

1916

Born on 16 September in Madurai, Tamil Nadu. "The initials before my name stand for the two influences of my life — M for my hometown, Madurai, and S for my mother, Shanmukhavadivu," Subbulakshmi would say.

1920s

Grows up humming the tunes of her mother's veena and of the nadaswaram from the Meenakshi Temple nearby. Later, experts are surprised at how her singing uncannily echos the glides and styles of these two instruments.

Learns Carnatic classical music from the famous singer, Semmangudi Srinivasa Iyer.

Stops schooling in Class 5. Practises music for hours, tuning the tambura, and her voice to it, to hone her ear and perfect her notes.

Cuts her first record at age 10 with the Columbia Gramophone Company, her mother playing the veena.

Gives her debut performance in 1927 at a concert in the 100-pillar hall of Tiruchirappalli's Rockfort Temple.

1930s

In 1932, her mother manages to get her a chance to sing at the Kumbakonam Mahamaham festival. She is so well received by both crowds and vidvans that she is asked to sing again in the prime evening slot.

In 1933, moves with her mother to Chennai, music captial of the South. On 28 December, makes her debut at a concert by the Indian Fine Arts Society.

Becomes a fixture in the city's music season. Sings at age 17 at the prestigious Madras Music Academy, which breaks tradition by allowing a teenager on stage. The famous veena player Sambasiva Iyer is said to have exclaimed, "Child, you carry a veena in your throat!"

Meets T. Sadasivam, advertising manager of the popular magazine *Ananda Vikatan*. To introduce her to a larger audience he encourages her to act and sing. She appears as 'Kokilagana Madurai M. S. Subbulakshmi' in *Sevasadanam*, a 1938 film based on a Munshi Premchand story with a bold social message.

By 1939, Music Academy needs the police to control crowds at her concert.

1940s

In 1940, stars in *Sakuntalai*, directed by American filmmaker Ellis Dungan who does not speak a word of Tamil! It also stars young Carnatic maestro G. N. Balasubramaniam, whose music influences MS.

Marries Sadasivam in 1940.

In 1944, Sadasivam, who is active in the freedom struggle, organises a series of fund-raising concerts for the Kasturba Memorial Trust. It is attended by top leaders of the day.

In 1945, does a landmark role in the musical film *Meera*, produced by Sadasivam. Its Hindi remake as *Meerabai* makes her well known across India.

Called "Suswaralakshmi Subbulakshmi" by Ustad Bade Ghulam Ali Khan, her concerts in Jalandhar, Jaipur, Bhopal and elsewhere draw large audiences, although she mainly sings Carnatic pieces by Tyagaraja and other composers in Telugu and Kannada.

Trains in Hindustani khayals, thumris and tappas from Siddheshwari Devi of Varanasi. Widens her repertoire — and reach — with bhajans in Hindi, Marathi, Gujarati and Bengali. The spiritual quality of her singing touches people the most.

1950s

Her fame grows. All her concerts are now for social causes. After one in 1953, in aid of Ramakrishna Mission, Delhi, Jawaharlal Nehru tells her, "Who am I, a mere prime minister, before the queen of song!"

Receives the Sangeet Natak Akademi Award in 1956.

1960s

Performs at the Edinburgh Music Festival in 1963, and in the UN General Assembly in 1966.

With more performances at some of the Festivals of India, she becomes the ambassador of Carnatic music overseas.

Records her first full length LP album 'Sri Venkateswara Suprabhatam' in 1963 for the Gramophone Company of India — still sells over 2 lakh copies a year in other formats.

In 1968, is the first female Carnatic musician to be given the Music Academy's Sangeetha Kalanidhi award.

1970s–80s

Sings at Carnegie Hall, New York, in 1977.

In 1982, gives a grand concert at Royal Albert Hall, London, to resounding applause.

Her last international concert is at the Festival of India at Paris in 1985.

1998

Awarded the Bharat Ratna.

2004

Passes away on 11 December. A fellow musician says in tribue, "Perfection is very hard to achieve and if anybody came close to it, it was M. S. Subbulakshmi."

সত্যজিৎ রায়

SATYAJIT RAY

1921–1992

Satyajit Ray was a product of the
Bengal Renaissance – multifaceted, multitalented,
and shaped by both East and West, tradition and modernity.
While his filmmaking was inspired by the neorealism in European
cinema, his films were about everyday India. They had ordinary people
and commonplace locations, but Ray's genius enabled audiences
to view them with a new awareness. When he entered the scene,
the Indian film industry was about half a century old, the 'alternative'
movement just beginning. His sophisticated artistry shot it into
the international limelight, influencing some of the
greatest filmmakers and changing the world's
view of Indian cinema.

WHEN SATYAJIT RAY was making his first and possibly most famous film, *Pather Panchali*, he kept running out of money. Not surprising, for producers were not convinced that a movie with no stars, no action, no dances or songs could possibly be a success. Instead, there were amateur actors, a young cinematographer who had never operated a film camera before, a director who had never ever directed a movie, and a script that seemed to be a series of drawings. Besides, the story of a poor family struggling to survive in rural Bengal sounded rather dull!

Ray did not give up. He pawned his wife's jewellery and sold his precious collection of music records for funds. Finally, the state government gave him a grant, believing the movie to be a documentary on community development! Three long years later, *Pather Panchali* ('Song of the Road') was released — a spare and poetic film with realistic settings, minimal dialogue and a gentle pace. It was as if viewers were witnessing the life of Apu, the central character, as it happened. But far from being boring, it was powerful and moving, leaving audiences stunned with its impact.

Pather Panchali won more than 15 national and international prizes. It is considered one of the greatest films ever made.

Ray was born into a prominent Bengali family — a deeply creative lot, who experimented with photography, and wrote poetry, books and music. His grandfather had set up a state-of-the-art printing press and published a children's magazine, *Sandesh*. His father, Sukumar Ray, famously wrote quirky nonsense verse, still popular today. Satyajit Ray himself, at various times in his life, was a graphic artist, designer, calligrapher, artist, editor, music composer and writer.

He avidly watched cinema from around the world, and was most impressed with some of the great American, French and Italian directors of the time. Particularly, he liked the ones with realistic settings, showcasing the lives of ordinary people. On a trip to London, he is said to have watched over a hundred films. One especially, *Bicycle Thieves* by the Italian director Vittorio de Sica, had a huge impact on him. By the time he returned to India, Ray had already decided that he wanted to turn the great Bengali novel, *Pather Panchali*, into a trilogy of films on the life of the young boy, Apu.

"I have travelled all around the world to see the rivers and the mountains, and I've spent a lot of money. I have gone to great lengths, I have seen everything. But I forgot to see just outside my house a dewdrop on a little blade of grass, a dewdrop which reflects in its convexity the whole universe around you."
Rabindranath Tagore, in young Ray's autograph book — an idea Ray goes on to reflect in his films

"A lesson I have learnt and have been at pains not to conceal is that filmmaking is by far the most physically demanding of all activities that is dignified by the epithet 'creative'. The whole process takes place in three broad stages: writing, filming, editing. All three are creative; while in the first and third one uses mainly one's head, the second calls for the use of all one's faculties — cerebral, physical and emotional — going full steam at all times."
Satyajit Ray

After the success of his first film, the first in the trilogy, Ray went on to make many more, teaching himself every aspect of the craft. He filmed, edited, designed sets by drawing elaborate sketches of each scene (some are collector's items today), composed music scores, wrote the credits in his special calligraphy fonts, designed the posters and costumes, and even helped with make-up!

His themes were usually on Bengali society and how changing times and clashing values affected individuals. His realistic technique was inspired by the great cinema of the time. But the soul of his films was his attention to detail. Seemingly ordinary, everyday scenes created unforgettable moments. His movies felt more like a finely finished piece of art that held your gaze. Or a beautiful poem you wanted to go back to over and over again. His characters spoke in Bengali, but his films spoke in the international language of cinema.

Ray's films received scores of awards from around the world during his lifetime. Most of them were stored in a trunk under his bed.

He was also a prolific author of children's books. In his grandfather's magazine, *Sandesh*, which he continued to edit and produce, he serialised his own detective story called *Feludar Goendagiri* ('Feluda's Sleuthing'). It featured Feluda, his teenaged cousin, and a comic crime-writer companion. The overwhelming response from both children and adults forced him to write a new Feluda book every year! In true Ray style, the stories did not just feature crime but action, travel, adventure, information about art, nature, literature and culture. Naturally, he illustrated them himself. His other popular figure was Professor Shonku, an eccentric, balding genius scientist-inventor who travelled to exotic locales around the world, taking his riveted readers along on adventures. Both characters have a cult-like following even today, with many of the stories adapted to films.

Considered one of the greatest directors ever, Satyajit Ray is placed along with international icons like Akira Kurosawa, Ingmar Bergman and Federico Fellini. His works continue to impact some of the best known names in cinema today. Hollywood director Martin Scorsese once said that he would never have become a filmmaker if he had not seen the Apu trilogy. The legendary Japanese filmmaker Kurosawa paid him the greatest tribute: "Not to have seen the cinema of Ray means existing in the world without seeing the sun or the moon."

"From his sketches and notes for his films, I see his sense of design, his obsession with detail which is visible in all his films. There is never an extra frame, never a superfluous image. Only a sense of perfect balance. In sketches of the costumes I see the care that goes into his use of colour; his orchestration of colour is painterly ... Colour is not merely an embellishment. it has great purpose; it has identity."
M. F. Husain

"I have learned a lot about India based on the works of remarkable Indian director Satyajit Ray, so it was my dream to make a film in his land. His viewpoint is very valuable to me and I love whatever he has done, so one of the main reasons behind making this film is my admiration for Satyajit Ray and his work."
Majid Majidi, on his 2017 film *Beyond the Clouds*

GOOPY GYNE
BAGHA BYNE

PATHER
PANCHALI

1921

Born on 2 May in Kolkata to a progressive Bengali Brahmo family fond of books, writing and music.

Grows up immersed in films and Western classical music. Wants to be a commercial artist.

1940s

After graduation from Presidency College in 1940, his mother persuades him to join family friend Tagore's Visva Bharati University in Shantiniketan.

Is strongly influenced by his teacher, artist Benod Behari Mukherjee, especially in attention to detail. Sketching trips to nearby villages are his first exposure to rural life. Also sees Oriental art closely — Indian, Japanese, Chinese. All of this impacts his filmmaking later.

In 1943, joins advertising agency D. J. Keymer as a visualiser. Works there for 13 years. Experiments with Indian motifs and calligraphy in ads. Creates new typefaces — later, his Ray Roman and Ray Bizarre win an international prize.

Begins to do book jackets for Signet Press in 1944. One is a version of Bibhutibhushan Bandopadhyay's *Pather Panchali*, which he reads for the first time. The idea of making a movie of it comes up.

Sets up the Calcutta Film Society with friends in 1947. Starts writing on cinema in English and Bengali for magazines. Tries adapting novels into screenplays.

In 1949, helps French filmmaker Jean Renoir with location scouting around Kolkata for *The River*. Renoir gives advice that Ray follows later: "You don't have to have too many elements in a film. But whatever you use must be the right elements, the expressive elements."

1950s

While working in London, sees Vittorio de Sica's *Bicycle Thieves*. Is captivated by its neo-realism — confirms his belief that it is possible to make realistic cinema shot on location, not studios, with unknown faces rather than stars. On the ship back home, finishes his script for *Pather Panchali*.

Spends 2 years looking for a producer before work begins on the film in 1952. Takes 3 years to finish.

Pather Panchali releases in Kolkata in 1955, and is a box-office hit. Has an international release at the Museum of Modern Art, New York, to many rave reviews.

It wins the President's Gold and Silver Medals. Also gets the special jury award for Best Human Document at the 1956 Cannes film festival.

Ray quits advertising to become a full-time filmmaker.

Aparajito, the second of the Apu triology, wins the Golden Lion award at the Venice Film Festival in 1957. *Apur Sansar*, the third, releases in 1959 with the debut of now famous actors Soumitro Chatterjee and Sharmila Tagore whom Ray handpicks.

1960s

Begins to make a film a year.

In 1961, revives the children's magazine *Sandesh*.

In 1964, makes the acclaimed *Charulata*, based on a Tagore novel. A bold, sensitive portrayal of womanhood, it is said to be his own favourite.

Feluda and Professor Shonku first appear in *Sandesh* in 1965. Both are inspired by Arthur Conan Doyle characters — Feluda by Sherlock Holmes, Shonku by Professor Challenger.

1970s

Makes his first non-Bengali feature film in 1970 — *Shatranj Ke Khiladi* in Hindi, based on Munshi Premchand's short story set on events before 1857.

In 1978, the Berlin Festival committee judges him one of the 3 all-time masters of cinema, with Ingmar Bergman and Charlie Chaplin. Oxford University honours him with a doctorate, an honour given before only to Chaplin.

1992

Releases his final film, *Agantuk*.

Presented an Honorary Oscar for Lifetime Achievement — the first for an Indian — recognising "his rare mastery of the art of motion pictures, and his profound humanism which has had an indelible influence on filmmakers and audiences throughout the world". Receives it in hospital.

The announcement of a Bharat Ratna award comes before he dies on 28 April.

"Who else can compete?" says his obituary in *The Independent*, UK.

মহাশ্বেতা দেবী

MAHASWETA DEVI

1926–2016

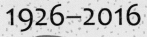

In spite of over a hundred novels
to her name, she could never be described
as just a writer. With her literary family and Shantiniketan
education, Mahasweta Devi's social and political awareness was
moulded early in life. Her future work held a mirror to society, startling
readers with her dark, stark image of the sufferings of the marginalised.
Living and working with the exploited tribals of Bengal and Bihar,
it was their stories she told, their battles for justice that she fought
through the one potent weapon she could wield – words.
To her, writing was activism.

THE STATUE STANDS in the middle of a busy traffic intersection in Ranchi, capital of Jharkhand. It is of a man, bare bodied, wearing only a dhoti and a turban. His gaze is intense. And there are iron shackles on his hands.

"Shackled? In free India?" asks Mahasweta Devi.

This is Birsa Munda. In the 1890s, in the areas that are now Jharkhand and Chhattisgarh, he led armed uprisings of tribals against landlords, moneylenders and the British Raj. These were the people who had forcibly taken over tribal land, crushing an ancient way of life. He is also the hero of Mahasweta Devi's famous book, *Aranyer Adhikar* ('Right to the Forest').

Mahasweta Devi was born into a highly literary Bengali family in Dhaka. Both her parents were writers and the extended family had an array of poets, artists, journalists and filmmakers. As a child, she spent long happy hours in a library of thousands of books maintained by her maternal grandmother. So no one was surprised when she chose to be a writer herself. What had them a bit baffled was the subjects she chose to write about.

Her first book, *Jhansir Rani* ('The Queen of Jhansi'), was about the legendary Rani Lakshmibai. Not content to research her book in the comfort of libraries, she got on a train and set out on a journey through Bundelkhand, where Lakshmibai had lived. She walked to far-flung villages, through rough terrain and in all kinds of weather, collecting folktales, legends and songs about the queen, even meeting descendants of those who had actually served her. Using this oral history, she wrote a unique book based on the memories of the people who lived on in the same land where the Rani had once ruled and fought her brave battles. This method of researching her work at the grassroots became her trademark.

Sometime in the 1960s, on a visit to Palamau in Bihar, she was horrified by what she saw. A rich landlord whose bullock could not pull a heavy cartload of paddy, yoked a labourer to the cart instead. The labourer pulled until his shoulder broke. The landlord was unapologetic. "He's only a bonded labourer," he said. As she travelled through the districts of Singhbhum and Hazaribagh, Mahasweta Devi began to see a depressing pattern.

"Once a tribal girl asked me, 'When we go to school, we read about Mahatma Gandhi. Did we have no heroes? Did we always suffer like this?' That is why I started writing about the tribal movements and the tribal heroes."

"I have always believed that the real history is made by ordinary people. I constantly come across the reappearance, in various forms, of folklore, ballads, myths and legends, carried by ordinary people across generations..."

"The reason and inspiration for my writing are those people who are exploited and used, and yet do not accept defeat ... Why should I look for my raw material elsewhere, once I have started knowing them? Sometimes it seems to me that my writing is really their doing."

Mahasweta Devi

The indigenous people, or tribals, had lived in the beautiful hills and forests of Central India since ancient times. They had a deep, spiritual attachment to their land — they took only as much as they needed, and shared equally amongst themselves. Eyeing their rich forest resources, the British changed the rules of land ownership. Suddenly, the tribals had their lands snatched away from them. Greedy landlords, traders and moneylenders moved in, exploiting their lack of education and simplicity. The forests that they had once fiercely protected were now devastated, rivers polluted and hills mined for minerals. Their social system was ripped apart, their gods, languages and arts lost. The once proud, self-sufficient tribes like the Mundas, Lodhas, Khedia Sabars and Dhikaros were now debt ridden and starving.

Years after Independence, Mahasweta Devi was horrified to find that the state still did not care about providing roads, employment, education or medical facilities to them. It was almost as if they did not exist. Deeply affected, she began to write about their problems, publishing her articles in newspapers and journals. She set up more than 30 organisations to fight for their rights.

Never one to do things halfway, she started living among the tribals in order to understand them better. They were guests in her house while she wrote petitions for them. She admired them for their dignity and lack of bitterness towards their exploiters. Instead, they accepted what came their way and hoped patiently for a better future.

Slowly, the displaced tribals, exploited women, bonded labourers, dying artists and artisans, and other downtrodden people began to find their way into Mahasweta Devi's writing. Her stories were of their oppression and exploitation but also of their rich history and traditions. Her language was a combination of Bengali and tribal dialects, and her style so blunt that it left her readers shaken.

She carried on her activism right into her late 80s, writing more than a hundred books and scores of articles, drawing the country's attention to the "curtain of darkness" that hid the exploited and neglected on the margins of society.

Until finally, the authorities removed the shackles from Birsa Munda's statue.

"It was difficult to say when she would start singing and render an entire [film] song ... It was impossible to predict when in the middle of the most polite conversation ... she would curtly dismiss civility and tell the person that he was a fraud. The station and degree of someone did not deter her. But, it was her innocence that stood out the most ... She combined humility and an unbreakable determination, simplicity of words and complexity of ideas, leaving those who listened to her completely changed."

G. N. Devy, scholar and cultural activist, 2016

"This is truly the age where the joota [shoe] is Japani, patloon [pants] is Englistani, the topi [hat] is Roosi [Russian], But the dil... dil [heart] is always Hindustani ... My country – torn, tattered, proud, beautiful, hot, humid, cold, sandy, shining India. My country."

Mahasweta Devi

The Queen of Jhansi

mahasweta devi
MOTHER OF 1084
TRANSLATED BY SAMIK BANDYOPADHYAY

mahasweta devi
DUST ON THE
ROAD
EDITED, TRANSLATED AND INTRODUCED
BY MAITREYA GHATAK

mahasweta devi
THE BOOK OF THE
HUNTER
TRANSLATED BY SAGAREE
AND MANDIRA SENGUPTA

Birsa Munda

অরণ্যের
অধিকার

মহাশ্বেতা

WRITE TO FIGHT

1926

Born on 14 January in Dhaka, now Bangladesh, to a liberal family of book lovers and writers. Is a fluent reader herself by age 4, books her favourite pastime.

As a child in Medinipur, Bengal, often cycles down to the edge of a forest where the Santhals live. Learns early how cultured, civilised and advanced they are. Sees them regularly harassed by authority just for being tribal.

1930s

Goes to school in Dhaka, Shantiniketan and Kolkata. While doing her intermediate at Ashutosh College, Kolkata, starts a block-printing and dyeing venture. "I was always over-energetic," she says.

1940s

Returns to Shantiniketan for her BA. Starts writing for the well known magazine *Desh*.

Joins Calcutta University in 1946 for an MA in English.

In 1947, marries playwright Bijon Bhattacharya, a founder of the Indian People's Theatre Association. Their son is born the next year.

In serious need of money, gets involved in a deal to export 15,000 monkeys to the US for medical trials, not realising that it's wrong! Luckily, the plan does not go through.

Gets a government job but is thrown out because her husband is a communist. In this very difficult period she realises "how it feels when one is hungry".

1950s

Contributes light stories to the journal *Sachitra Bharat,* getting Rs 15 per story — a lot at that time.

Her first book *Jhansir Rani,* releases in 1953, marking her as a very original writer.

1960s

Starts teaching English literature in 1964 at the Bijoygarh Jyotish Roy College for poorer students.

Gets more and more immersed in tribal and village life. Now writes regularly about these issues as a roving reporter for the newspaper *Jugantor*. Also begins to write crime stories.

Becomes a rural reporter for the Bengali dailies *Bortoman* and *Aajkal* as well, covering social oppression.

1970s

In 1974, publishes *Hajar Churashir Maa* ('Mother of 1084'), one of her best known books, about the brutal suppression of the Naxal movement. It is later adapted for theatre and made into a Hindi film.

Her famous account of police violence on an illiterate tribal rebel woman, Dopdi, appears in the collection *Agnigarbha* in 1978. This powerful retelling of Draupadi in *Mahabharata* is written in one night.

Takes over her father's magazine *Bortika* after he dies in 1979. Gets tribals to write their life stories in it so they are heard straight from the grassroots. They also become her subscribers, about 2000 of them from Medinipur alone.

Aranyer Adhikar ('Right of the Forest'), her novel about Birsa Munda, the tribal activist, wins her the Sahitya Akademi Award. Now she has complete acceptance among the tribals who see her as their voice.

"I feel that people have played games with the tribals," she says. An 1871 British law had 'notified' certain tribes as suspect, assuming they had criminal tendencies. Though 'denotified' in 1952, they are still harassed. With land taken away for 'development', they are also poor.

1982

Closely associated from now on with the Purulia Khedia Sabar Kalyan Samiti. She often walks 25 km a day in the forests, interacting with tribals. Her only children's story in English, *The Why-Why Girl*, comes out of this connection.

1990s

In 1996, wins the Jnanpith Award, India's highest literary prize.

Jokes that a major body of her work will remain unpublished — her large number of letters to ministers, complaints, petitions and pleas on behalf of tribals!

Takes up the police killing in 1998 of Budhan Sabar of the Sabar Khedia tribe. Sets up the Denotified Tribes and Communities Rights Action Group with tribal activists Ganesh Devy and Lakshman Gaekwad.

2000s

Awarded the Padma Vibhushan in 2006.

In 2007, leads a protest of artists and intellectuals against the state's appropriation of land for factories in Singur and Nandigram, West Bengal.

In a fitting finale, a month before she passes away in 2016, her constant campaigning leads to the unshackling of Birsa Munda's statue in Ranchi. "[T]he tribals are the last word of my life," she once says.

सुंदरलाल बहुगुना

SUNDERLAL BAHUGUNA

born 1927

He walked hundreds of kilometres,

talking to people, raising awareness about the

rapid destruction of the fragile Himalayan ecosystem.

A Gandhian and freedom fighter, he and his wife spent decades

doing grassroots work for social upliftment in the villages of Uttarakhand.

One of the spearheads of the unique Chipko movement, this man of

the mountains, Sunderlal Bahuguna, has pledged his life to them.

Now in his 90s, he continues to inspire new generations of

environmental activists with his mantra, the 5F Formula –

'Grow trees for Food, Fodder, Fertiliser, Fibre and Fuel'.

IN A REMOTE HIMALAYAN VILLAGE, a little boy watched quietly as his mother worked. She woke up at the crack of dawn to light the kitchen fire, cook a simple meal and leave fodder for the cows. Then with a group of women, she walked into the forest to gather firewood. The heavy load on her head, she stopped to pick mushrooms, roots and herbs for the cooking pot. After grazing the animals and weeding the fields, it was time to trek the long distance to the water source, wash clothes and carry buckets of water back home. She worked for more than 18 hours a day, every day. One night, after everyone had gone to sleep, the boy heard his mother sigh in exhaustion, "Oh god, give me death."

That was the night Sunderlal Bahuguna decided he was going to do something to ease the burden of women like his mother, women who worked so hard to keep their families comfortable and the village economy thriving.

As a 13-year-old in the village of Maroda, near Tehri, Uttarakhand, he was deeply impressed by the Gandhian, Sridev Suman. From him, he learnt how to fight for just causes through non-violence and satyagraha. His budding political career came to an end when he met and married Bimla Behn, a social activist. They moved to a distant village and set up the Silyara Ashram, where they took up causes affecting the local people. The most important of these was teaching hill women how important they were to the village economy. Bahuguna always insisted that since the women did most of the farming and animal husbandry, "we [men] are the runners and messengers — the real leaders are the women."

At this time, he noticed how deforestation was affecting the beautiful Himalayan hills. Timber mills and commercial foresters were stripping entire hillsides of trees. Roads and hydro-electric projects were adding to the devastation. There were more landslides, less clean water, lower agricultural yields, and floods.

In these isolated hill villages, people rely on forests for food, employment and trade. And yet, they were being denied access to them. In one area, the locals were stopped from cutting trees for their agricultural tools but the same forest was allotted to a sports goods manufacturer for commercial use! The villagers could only watch in increasing alarm as their most precious resource was being destroyed before their eyes. How could they fight these powerful outsiders?

"Initially, I believed politics was a way to make a substantial change in society. But Bimla inspired me to look deeper. With her support and the guidance of a few others, I realised that to make a real change, I would need to step out from my bubble and live among the masses in the rural and remote parts of the country. I needed to understand their everyday issues and whether at all government policies helped them."

Sunderlal Bahuguna

"The brilliance of Sunderlalji lay in how he communicated about his life in the village at the national and international level. He was a journalist by profession, after all, and wrote columns for many papers. When he was not busy with his padyatras, he was writing. His writings on Chipko are unforgettable."

Vandana Shiva, environmental activist. 2016

By using a most unusual tactic. Hugging trees.

And the Chipko movement was born. Chipko means 'to stick'. Women formed groups and literally stuck to the trees, daring the contractors to "axe us, not the trees". Whenever tree-cutters arrived, a messaging system run by Bahuguna and his fellow activists alerted them to gather together and thwart the cutters. Uncaring of threats, they sang: "What do the forests bear? Soil, water and pure air. Soil, water and pure air sustain the earth and all she bears." The contractors and even local policemen were stunned by this non-violent protest and retreated in confusion!

Bahuguna started a series of foot marches to spread this peaceful and powerful message from village to village through folk songs and stories. His padyatra had a massive national impact. Tree felling was banned for 15 years. And, in an era where there was no social media or even decent phone networks, similar Chipko movements sprung up in other parts of India. From the Vindhyas to the Western Ghats, it compelled governments to sit up and take notice.

The people were making their demands known — respect for their local culture and ecology, sustainable practices and a stake in their own future.

Bahuguna considers himself the guardian of the Himalayan ecology. So when the mega Tehri Dam project on the Bhagirathi River was proposed, he jumped to the challenge. The dam is set in a pristine and fragile ecosystem, prone to earthquakes, and would destroy thousands of villages and farmlands, displacing more than 85,000 people for the sake of water and electricity for faraway Delhi.

Bahuguna went to court, was arrested, and finally went on hunger strike at Mahatma Gandhi's samadhi for almost 75 days! The government was forced to set up a review committee. But this time, the dam lobbies were too powerful. In 2004, Sunderlal and Bimla Behn were forcibly evicted to government built accommodation when their house was flooded out by the rising dam waters.

But just like the promise he made to his mother all those years ago, Bahuguna has vowed never to give up the fight for a fair and sustainable economy for all.

"In the Chipko movement we had to fight for eight years to make the truth known to the government that the main product of the Himalayan forests is not timber but water."

"So I raise the question, how long will this dam work? It is temporary. But if they plant the whole Himalaya with trees, the water renewing capacity of Himalaya will increase. And that will be permanent. It will make the hill people prosperous also. Today what has happened to the hills by felling the trees is that there are landslides and the soil … is flowing down to the sea. And do you know, there is an ecological rule that men follow their soil. The people are going to the plains."
Sunderlal Bahuguna

"Among other things, the Chipko movement was also one of the first movements in India which witnessed an uprising of women. Women from villages, who usually spend their lives indoors, stepped out with the weapon of compassion to protect mother nature. It was extremely empowering."
Bimla Bahuguna

Sustain the earth and all she bears

Bimla Behn

EARTH WARRIOR

1927

Born on 9 January in Maroda village, near Tehri, Uttarakhand.

1940s–50s

Gandhian social activist and freedom fighter Sridev Suman comes to his village. Intrigued by the message of non-violence, satyagraha and serving the common people, young Bahuguna wants to join "the army of Gandhi". Writes and distributes information, orgainses protests, even goes to jail.

At 18, goes to study at the Sanatan Dharam College in Lahore. Does well in studies, and is politically active.

Returns to Tehri in 1947. Stands for election to the Tehri Constituent Assembly. Loses but becomes a district general secretary of the Congress.

Starts a fight against untouchability. Opens the Thakkar Bapa hostel where students of all castes live together.

Meets Gandhi's disciple Mira Behn, and is impressed by her work for rural development in the Bhilangana Valley.

In 1956, marries Bimla, follower of another Gandhi disciple, Sarala Behn. Quits politics and they set up the Silyara Ashram in a small village. They motivate the locals to construct canals and roads, and fight liquor addiction.

1960s

Vinoba Bhave tells him to go on a padyatra, a foot march, through the Himalayas to educate people about Gram Swaraj — self-reliant village societies. Bahuguna covers more than 5,700 km through forests and hills. Notices the damage caused by big developmental projects in the Himalayas.

1970s

In 1970, deforestation leads to a landslide near Badrinath and devastating floods of the Alaknanda River — a major wake-up call to check reckless tree felling and big projects.

Bahuguna begins to drum up awareness and support for non-violent protests against tree cutting. Small groups have already started to agitate.

The first important move is in 1973. In Mandal village, Chandi Prasad Bhatt leads a protest against the allotment of 300 trees to Symonds, a manufacturer of sporting goods in Allahabad, Uttar Pradesh.

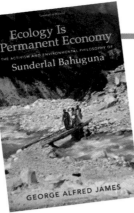

In 1974, the men of Reni village are deliberately diverted elsewhere while contractors arrive. Gaura Devi leads a band of 27 women, who finally take to hugging the trees to protect them, in a 4-day standoff. The Chipko movement is born.

It spreads quickly across Uttarakhand. The main leaders are Sunderlal Bahuguna, Gaura Devi, Chandi Prasad Bhatt, the poet Ghanasyam Raturi and Dhoom Singh Negi. But what marks it is the participation of women. The Bishnoi women of Rajasthan too had hugged khejri trees to save them, way back in 1730.

Bahuguna's slogan "Ecology is permanent economy" becomes famous. Meets British forester Richard St Barbe Baker in 1977, who takes the Chipko message international.

1980s

Meets the prime minister, Indira Gandhi, in 1980. Gets a 15-year ban on chopping green trees in the Himalayas.

Nominated for and turns down the Padma Shri in 1981.

Goes on a 300-day, 4780-km march through the Himalayas from Kashmir to Kohima to build support for the movement to save the hills.

In 1983, his follower Panduranga Hegde starts the Appiko (Kannada for 'chipko') movement in Karnataka.

Gets active in the Beej Bachao Andolan, to save seeds.

In 1987, the Chipko movement wins the Right Livelihood Award, known as the Alternative Nobel.

1990s

Work restarts with the mega Tehri Dam on Bhagirathi River. Bahuguna is completely opposed to it, as are several experts. "A river is a full ecosystem. It is not only the water," he says.

Protests and talks continue. Goes on an awareness raising cycle tour in 1991, from the mouth of the Ganga in the Bay of Bengal to Gaumukh. A major earthquake in the dam region at this time proves it is in a seismic belt.

In 1995, goes on two long fasts for 45 and 75 days. There are government assurances and a 10-year long Supreme Court case.

2000s

In 2004, the dam finally does come up. Water floods entire villages and his home. Forced to relocate, he says, "Our history, geography, culture, everything is drowning."

Awarded the Padma Vibhushan in 2009.

"My fight is to save the Himalayas, and it will continue ... Truth never dies," he still believes.

அருணா ராய்

ARUNA ROY

born 1946

Working in a small village in Rajasthan,
Aruna Roy realised how little of democracy's promised
'people power' filtered down to those who needed it most – the poor.
They could ask no questions of the government, not even about what was
due to them by right. Determined to take on this "culture of secrecy",
she and her fellow travellers, as she calls them, started on a long
journey to demand government transparency and the people's
right to know. It led to the Right to Information Act that now,
finally, empowers the common man. Someone said,
free India's history will one day be defined
as pre- and post-RTI.

WHAT DOES A YELLOW WALL have to do with democracy?

A bright sunny yellow with shiny red columns. The sarpanch is proud of the newly painted wall of her panchayat office. Filling the columns are some rather humdrum details — work to be done by the panchayat, funds granted, materials used, contractors' names... But for the villagers, these figures are an important victory. They are public records telling them how money for their welfare is being spent, information previously hidden in locked files. But few know that this wall came about after a long struggle by a remarkable lady and her team.

In the household where Aruna Roy grew up, grumbling was not an option. If you felt something was wrong, you had to find a way to fix it. She learnt early to have the moral and physical courage to jump in and fight when she sensed injustice. After a stellar academic career, she entered the Indian Administrative Service. Six years later, she created a minor storm amongst her friends and family when she resigned. Why would she give up this much-coveted job? She had decided that she wanted to help the underprivileged in a different, more direct way.

Aruna went to Tilonia, Rajasthan, where her husband, Sanjit 'Bunker' Roy had established what is known as the Barefoot College. Living with the villagers, they saw their problems first hand and helped solve them in practical ways.

A few years later, she moved to the village of Devdungri with her colleagues Shankar Singh and Nikhil Dey. There, in a modest mud hut, they set up the Mazdoor Kisan Shakti Sangathan (MKSS). Their main aim was to help the villagers understand and use their democratic rights to improve their lives.

It began with a fight for minimum wages. Desperately poor villagers worked up to eight hours a day on government sponsored public works which promised a minimum daily wage. But when they asked for their money, their names were mysteriously missing from the panchayat records. Or, they would be given an amount far less than entitled by government rules. It was obvious that the rest was being pocketed by corrupt officials. When the labourers asked to see the receipts and records, they were told these were "secret". Greedy landlords often claimed ownership of vast areas of village land that did not really belong to them. These records were also "secret".

Aruna and her MKSS team swung into action.

"[T]here are two kinds of power: the power of the people and the power of the system. Both have to acknowldege and recognise each other ... the Constitution gives me equality. I believe that equality is fundamental to existence, and this sense of equality is there in so many ordinary Indians. That's what the RTI is all about."
Aruna Roy

"Soon after the RTI Act came into force, parents in Panchampur village in the district of Banda, Uttar Pradesh, used it to track their local school teacher, who rarely made an appearance ... After learning from RTI activists that they could seek attendance and leave records of the government school teacher, 15 villagers filed an application asking about his whereabouts, and also questioned the responsibility of the Primary Education Department ... Immediate action was taken: a new school teacher was appointed to the village school, and an enquiry was ordered against the absconder."
Betwa Sharma, journalist, 2015

They organised a series of hunger strikes outside record offices, demanding to see the expenditure records. The authorities were taken aback at being questioned but ignored the protestors. The MKSS changed tactics. Using a blend of catchy local tunes, songs, theatre and slogans, they began to raise awareness and connect with the public, telling them it was their right to ask for public accounts. "Hamara paisa, hamara hisaab," the villagers chanted. The movement spread and, as awareness built up, Aruna managed to organise Jan Sunvais, public hearings, where officials were asked why they could not reveal public documents like land and work records.

Meanwhile, other shocking facts began to tumble out. 'Completed' projects like dispensaries, schools and community centres turned out to simply not exist. When the villagers demanded to see the documents of such works, officials fobbed them off with excuses like, "The cows have eaten them!"

Despite threats and intimidation, the MKSS decided to step up the game and take the fight to the state capital, Jaipur. A Rajasthan government order finally went out stating that panchayat records should be painted on information boards for all to see. And that copies of records should be handed over within four days of an application. However, it did not always work that way. Demands for records were stalled. And one gram sewak even ran away with the original records, not to be be traced for days!

The MKSS was making a point: democracy was not just about casting a vote. Elected representatives had to be answerable to citizens — and that included sharing information. 'Shared information is shared power' was their slogan.

This was the beginning of the Right to Information campaign for transparent governance. It snowballed as activists from other parts of the country joined in. Their demand was a *law* that made information a right for all citizens.

After almost 15 years of struggle, the path-breaking Right to Information Bill was finally passed by parliament. Apart from guarding against corruption and misgovernance, the RTI Act reminded every citizen, even the poorest and most marginalised, that even they could influence decisions at the highest level. And it reminded the government that it was their democratic duty to be accountable and responsive to citizens' needs.

"In 2010, K. S. Sagaria smelt a rat when the paperwork showed that seven ponds had been constructed for below poverty lines families in Kushmal village of Odisha, but no one in the village could spot them.

So he filed an RTI application which revealed that the ponds were never dug, the 'labourers' who worked to 'construct' the ponds included dead people.

Following complaints, the administration suspended the officials involved in the subterfuge, and the project was renewed, but this time, the villagers vowed to keep a check on its progress."

Betwa Sharma, journalist, 2015

"I am aware that RTI has thrown me up as an icon but in actual fact so many people were part of it. It re-established my faith that democracy could work for people. It is the only politics that I can believe in ... By redistributing information you redistribute power."

Aruna Roy

MKSS

Right to Information Act, 2005

1. Short title, extent and commencement.—

(1) This Act may be called the Right to Info
2005.

(2) It extends to the whole of India exce
Jammu and Kashmir.

(3) The provisions of sub-section (1)
sub-sections (1) and (2) of section 5
24, 27 and 28 shall come into forc
remaining provisions of this Act
one hundred and twentieth day

2. Definitions.—In this Act, u
requires,—

(a) "appropriate Governme
uthority which is establi
substantia

THE RIGHT TO DEMAND

1946

Born on 26 May into a free-thinking Tamil family. Grows up in Delhi.

1949–65

Of all the schools she goes to, she counts her 2 years in Kalakshetra, Chennai, as the most impactful — "As a 9-year-old, I saw women dancing on stage with men, breaking gender and caste barriers..."

Gets a master's in English literature from Delhi University.

1968

Joins the Indian Administrative Service (IAS), in the Tamil Nadu cadre. Soon moves to Delhi. Realises she wants to work more directly with the poor and the marginalised.

1974

Leaves the IAS and joins her husband at the Social Work and Research Centre, or Barefoot College, in Tilonia, Rajasthan, that he set up in 1972. Has her "schooling in grassroots work" there.

1987

Along with colleagues Nikhil Dey, Shankar Singh and others, she founds the Mazdoor Kisan Shakti Sangathan (MKSS), in the small village of Devdungri, Rajasthan, to empower workers and farmers. They discover that workers are not paid due wages under government schemes. When questioned, officials deny them information.

1990s

In 1994, MKSS starts a campaign for Jan Sunvais in Rajasthan, where officers can be questioned about public money matters. The first hearings throw up all kinds of misdeeds and corruption.

The catchy slogan 'Hamara paisa, hamara hisaab' ('our money, our accounts') comes from a barely literate woman who says, if she gives her son Rs 10 to buy things she has a right to ask for accounts — and it should be the same with the government. With around 60 per cent women in the movement, they form the backbone.

In 1996, a year after the government fails to make good its promise to open up files to people, MKKS organises a 40-day sit-in protest in Beawar, Ajmer, demanding access to records. About 150 villages give their support.

A new slogan for the Right to Information (RTI) movement — 'The right to know is the right to live' — comes from a strong editorial in *Jansatta* by journalist Prabhash Joshi.

MKSS launches the National Campaign for the People's Right to Information (NCPRI) with others, asking for a law giving right to information. "Demanding information is more than the framing of a question. It is an attack on the culture of secrecy," says Aruna.

The protests and struggle continue through the following years in Rajasthan, spreading to other parts of India. Eminent beauraucrats and lawyers explore legal and administrative ways to implement such a law in practice.

2000s

In 2004, Aruna is selected as a member of the National Advisory Council, a think tank with prominent members from all walks of life, set up to advise the UPA-1 government. Resigns after 3 years.

After 15 years of campaigning, on 15 June 2005 the Right to Information Act is passed unanimously by Parliament, providing citizens the licence to information from public authorities. More than 80 lakh RTI applications are now filed every year, showing how necessary it was.

The National Rural Employment Guarantee Act (NREGA) is passed the same year, promising every rural household 100 days of work a year at minimum wages.

But with attacks mounting on RTI users — and around 70 killed already — the next step is to bring in laws to protect whistleblowers and redress grievances, for which MKKS is campaigning with the NCPRI.

Aruna continues to be involved with Right to Food, pensions for workers in the unorganised sector, and taking forward her cherished project Loktantrashala, the School for Democracy, near Ajmer in Rajasthan.

THE RTI STORY
POWER TO THE PEOPLE

ARUNA ROY with the MKSS Colle
Foreword by GOPALKRISHNA GA

PHOTO CREDITS

Rabindranath Tagore

p 11: Painting 'Head Study' © National Gallery of Modern Art, New Delhi/IndiaPicks.com

p 11: Nobel Prize medal © Jonathunder/Wikimedia Commons

p 12: *Stray Birds* book cover © Cosimo Classics/Amazon.in

p 12: *Gitanjali* book cover © Fingerprint! Publishing/Amazon.in

p 12: *Gora* book cover © Roman Books/Amazon.in

p 12: *Sanchayita* book cover © Ashok Books/Amazon.in

p 13: *My Reminiscences* book cover © Macmillan/OpenLibrary.org

p 13: *Riddle Plays* book cover © ExoticIndiaArt.com

p 13: *Children's Tagore* book cover © Oxford University Press/Amazon.in

p 13: Painting 'Face' © National Gallery of Modern Art, New Delhi/IndiaPicks.com

Rakhmabai

p 17: Queen Victoria © Alexander Bassano/Wikimedia Commons

p 17: Glass jars © J&D Trading Co., Bluemaize.net, Tverd.info

p 18: *Doctor Rakhmabai* movie poster © IMDB.com

p 18: 'End child marriage' poster © UNICEF

p 19: Rakhmabai's letter © Agents of Ishq

Mahatma Gandhi

p 23: Khadi cotton scarf © Maiwa Handprints Ltd.

p 25: *The Story of My Experiments with Truth* book cover © Fingerprint! Publishing/Amazon.in

p 25: *Inspiring Thoughts* book cover © Rajpal Publishing/Amazon.in

p 25: Commemorative stamp on 100 Years of Mahatma Gandhi's return © Postagestamps.gov.in

Periyar E. V. Ramasamy

p 29: *Kudi Arasu* magazine © Roja Muthaiah Research Library/Wikimedia Commons

p 30: *Periyar* book cover © Rupa Publications India/Amazon.in

p 30: *Pen Aen Adimaiyanaal?* book cover © Bharathi Puthakalayam/Amazon.in

p 31: Dog © ForwardPress.in

p 31: Dravidar Kazhagam flag © World Atheist Conference 2018

Begum Rokeya

p 35: *The Indian Ladies' Magazine* © WeChanged.ugent.be

p 36: Begum Rokeya University building © Bishalprontoroy/Wikimedia Commons

p 36: Begum Rokeya University logo © Brur.ac.bd

p 37: *Sultana's Dream* book cover © The Feminist Press/Amazon.in

p 37: *A Feminist Foremother* book cover © Orient BlackSwan/Amazon.in

Subramania Bharati

p 41: Bharati with his wife Chellamma © madeinthoughts.com/Wikimedia Commons

p 41: *Vijaya* magazine © Fowler & Fowler/Wikimedia Commons

p 41: *Swadesamitran* © BharathiPayilagam.blogspot.com

p 41: Commemorative stamp © TamilAndVedas.com

p 41: *India* magazine © Tamil Journalism/Wordpress

p 41: Goddess Saraswati © FindMessages.com

p 43: *Subramania Bharati – Selected Poems* book cover © Hachette India/Amazon.in

p 43: *Bharatiar Kavithaigal* book cover © Dr. S. Vijaya Bharati/Amazon.in

p 43: 'Bharatiar Songs' album cover © Rajkumar Bharathi/Kosmik

p 43: *Bharatiar Katturaigal* book cover © CreateSpace Independent Publishing/Amazon.in

C. V. Raman

p 47: Lenin Prize medal © Ivtorov/Wikimedia Commons

p 47: Raman Effect diagram © Arne M Vandenbroucke/ResearchGate.net

p 47: Mridangam © Domtw/Wikimedia Commons

p 48: Diamond atom structure © UCL/Flickr

p 49: Professor C. V. Raman teaching © Rediff.com

p 49: Bharat Ratna © Kumar Rajendran/Wikimedia Commons

Jawaharlal Nehru

p 53: Nehru-Gandhi family group photo © NehruMemorial.nic.in/Wikimedia Commons

p 53: Nehru signing the Indian Constitution © Shersinghstyle.wordpress.com/Wikimedia Commons

p 53: Nehru, Gandhi and Patel AICC 1946 © Kulwant Roy/Wikimedia Commons

p 53: Nehru signature © Connormah/Wikimedia Commons

p 53: Children © bri vos/Wikimedia Commons

p 54: Nehru with children © Photodivison.gov.in

p 55: *Toward Freedom* book cover © The John Day Co/Archive.org

p 55: *The Discovery of India* book cover © Penguin India/Amazon.in

p 55: *Glimpses of World History* book cover © WorthPoint

p 55: Rose © Ncxsqld.com

Babasaheb Ambedkar

p 59: Ambedkar with the drafting committee of the Indian Constitution © Sandesh Hiwale/Wikimedia Commons

p 59: Constitution of India © Loc.gov/Wikimedia Commons

p 60: *Buddha or Karl Marx* book cover © Dr. Bhimrao Ambedkar/Amazon.in

p 61: *The Untouchables* book cover © Samyak Prakashan/Amazon.in

p 61: *Riddle of Rama and Krishna* book cover © Mythri Books/KeralaBookStore.com

p 61: *Annihilation of Caste* book cover © Navayana/Amazon.in

p 61: *Ambedkar: Autobiographical Notes* book cover © Campfire Books/Amazon.in

p 61: Tobby the dog © Frontline/Wikimedia Commons

P. C. Mahalanobis

p 65: Desktop computer © Lamune-commonswiki/Wikimedia Commons

p 65: Early computer © Archive.org

p 66: Padma Vibhushan © Auckland War Memorial Museum/Wikimedia Commons

p 67: Commemorative stamp © India Post/Wikimedia Commons

p 67: Mahalanobis Distance diagram © Laila Poisson/ResearchGate.net

Satyendra Nath Bose

p 71: Cardboard box © Amazon.in

p 71: Esraj © Eastern Music Instruments/Blogspot

p 72: Crystallography © Bensaccount/Wikimedia Commons

p 73: *The Principle of Relativity* book cover © Andesite Press/Amazon.in

p 73: Bose-Einstein Condensate © National Institute of Standards and Technology/Wikimedia Commons

C. K. Nayudu

p 77: 1932 Indian Test Cricket team © Unknown/Wikimedia Commons

p 77: Cricket ball © Marie-Lan Nguyen/Wikimedia Commons

In appreciation . . .

Writing this book has been an inspirational journey – reacquainting myself with these great visionaries, marvelling at their sheer grit, hard work and wisdom.

The other great joy was being able to work with the fantastic Tulika team again! Radhika Menon and Deeya Nayar are game changers themselves, book navigators par excellence and generous editors without whom none of this would even exist. My grateful thanks to them all.

A heartfelt thanks to Aparna Chivukula and Roshni Pochont for the beautiful, distinctive collages and other images that capture the essence of each game changer.

I owe my loving family – Chit, Vallari and Chengis – a huge debt of gratitude for their helpful suggestions, supplies of tea and stationery during the writing of this book. It will, of course, be paid off sometime soon in fudge brownies!